DOLL MAKING

DOLL MAKING
A CREATIVE APPROACH

JEAN RAY LAURY

PHOTOGRAPHS BY GAYLE SMALLEY

VNR VAN NOSTRAND REINHOLD COMPANY
NEW YORK CINCINNATI TORONTO LONDON MELBOURNE

Van Nostrand Reinhold Company Regional Offices:
New York Cincinnati Chicago Millbrae Dallas
Van Nostrand Reinhold Company International Offices:
London Toronto Melbourne

Drawings by the author
Photography by Gayle Smalley except where otherwise indicated
Designed by Rosa Delia Vasquez
Type set by V & M Typographical, Inc.
Printed by Halliday Lithograph Corporation
Color printed by Bridge Litho Co., Inc.
Bound by Complete Books Company

Published by Van Nostrand Reinhold Company
450 West 33rd Street, New York, N.Y. 10001
Published simultaneously in Canada by
Van Nostrand Reinhold Company Ltd.

16 15 14 13 12 11 10 9 8 7 6 5 4 3 2 1

Foreword

It was with immense delight that I learned of this book on fabric dolls by Jean Ray Laury. Mrs. Laury has not only proven herself a communicative author in her previous book, *Appliqué Stitchery*, but she is also one of California's finest craftsmen in her own right. Further, reflecting on the contents of this book, I realized that absolutely nothing else in folk art can have the universal appeal that dolls have.

Man has always been involved, since the first cave drawings, in reproducing the human form. A child's first drawings are generally attempts at creating human forms. His first images show enlarged faces, with sticks for arms, feet and torso. Facial expressions, without words, can convey everything in human emotions. It is a mother's face that an infant first studies in order to gain security. The human form is the main preoccupation of artists the world over. Why? Because man needs to identify himself in the universe for reasons of security and self-knowledge. One of the best ways to learn about an indigenous group of people is by studying its self-image as reflected in its dolls.

As director of a folk art and craft gallery, I have given much thought to a working definition of the term "folk art." I feel that it is an art form which is spontaneous, traditional, anonymous, functional and lacking in self-consciousness. Above all, it is to me the best way a people can reach out and touch me; can force me to "see" them.

Doll forms, created by artists, reflect the spirit of a people better than anything else, whether created by folk artists or contemporary craftsmen.

This collection of dolls and their makers should give us insight, sometimes humorous, sometimes shocking, but always revealing.

Edith R. Wyle
Director
The Egg and The Eye Gallery

Dedication

For Lizabeth, Alison, Hilary Jean, Kristi, Jeannie, Natalie, Jo Anne, Rachel, Alison, Jenny, Elise, Nell Jean, Suerie, Bari, Lisa, Elise, Joell, Karen and Brenda—who all love dolls.

Acknowledgments

With my sincere thanks to the doll makers everywhere who inspired my work and who generously loaned their dolls, and to Gayle Smalley, photographer; Barbara Klinger, editor; and Frank B. Laury, reader-critic, for their special talents.

Contents

FOREWORD

1. ABOUT DOLLS   8

2. SIMPLE DOLLS   18

3. SINGLE-SHAPE DOLLS   24

4. JOINTED DOLLS   38

5. ARCH-SHAPED DOLLS   62

6. PILLOW DOLLS   72

7. TRANSFERRING CHILDREN'S IDEAS INTO DOLLS   78

8. FACES & HAIR   86

9. STOCKING-FACE DOLLS   98

10. KNITTED & WOVEN DOLLS   108

11. OTHER MATERIALS FOR DOLLS   116

12. OTHER DIRECTIONS   130

1.

ABOUT DOLLS

Plate 1. "Doll" by the author. 16 inches high. Stuffed and hand-sewn felt with felt appliqué.

Plate 2. "Girl with Braids" by Kathy Fukami Glascock of Los Angeles, Calif. Papier-mâché head with body of stuffed fabric. (Photo by Baylis Glascock.)

About Dolls

Dolls have attracted the interest of museums and individual collectors throughout the world. But few collections and few books written about dolls give any serious attention to the "rag doll," the homemade fabric doll. These dolls are made, used, loved and lost. Many are simply worn out. They are of little or no monetary value to collectors. But to those who make them, these dolls have a far more important worth, for they offer an opportunity to exercise individual creativity using simple materials and methods that give free play to the imagination. So, while homemade fabric dolls carry no identifying marks to assure "authenticity" or date of manufacture, each carries its creator's personality and offers the collector insight into the nature of the individual who made it and of the person who used it.

This book is essentially for those persons who are interested in exploring doll making in all its forms. Though the emphasis is on dolls made in part or entirely of fabric, many other crafts besides needlework are involved and persons with skills in other artistic media will find it a challenge to apply their talents to doll making. The examples in this book are a cross section of what is being done today. They show the basic principles of doll making as well as the new directions being pursued which go beyond the framework of this tradition.

In doll making there are no illusions of grandeur or greatness, and few pretensions. Dolls consist simply of cloth, some stuffing, a measure of imagination, certainly persistence, and, most important of all, an awareness of human qualities. That dolls often have an import that exceeds the humble nature of their materials attests to the creative potential within the gamut of the doll-making process.

What intrigues us most about a doll is not the surface appearance, but what lurks behind that appearance—that essence of a human quality which a doll can bring to our attention. As in any art form, the ultimate value of the work depends upon the perceptive and expressive abilities of the artist.

Humans have a natural inclination to make images. Dolls are manifestations of this propensity expressed in three-dimensional form. Within its scope, doll making has many different possibilities. One of these includes dolls which are the spontaneous products of traditional folk art. Second, there are dolls produced as toys, playthings for children. And third, there are dolls which, through personal and aesthetic statements, make an effort to communicate.

Thus dolls are sometimes created as folk art, sometimes as toys, and sometimes as sculptural forms. As folk art, dolls continue a well-established tradition. Folk artists have always expressed themselves in an unassuming and sometimes naïve way. In dolls this leads to an easily comprehended portrayal of human traits that may be shared by everyone. There is no place for the esoteric or snobbish in doll making. The work is unhampered by artificial rules or styles of acceptability. Dolls have a universal appeal, and we respond to them as we do to the representation of the human form in other media.

Dolls as a folk art do not seem endangered by commercialization. There is too little commercial value in the single handmade doll for anyone to create such work for reasons other than the pleasure derived from it. Certainly more advanced and sophisticated dolls are available. But the handmade ones thrive, and perhaps that is why they do not often survive. Dolls that are handled, used, or played with get worn out.

Dolls as toys achieve a delightful likeness to humans. The re-creation of characteristics of personality is more essential than any portrait accuracy in dolls. Anatomical "correctness" is of little concern, as most dolls possess a kind of endearing awkwardness and a humble spirit. The materials too are humble; the methods are available within every home, and the statements are so direct that we are captivated by them. Mothers make dolls for their children to play with as dolls were made for them. The materials change; the purpose does not.

Our national acceptance of obsolescence may make us forget the handcrafts in a mass-production technology. But as long as there are children, there will be a place for rag dolls. The best-loved dolls of children are those which provide some basis on which the imagination can feed. If everything is there (the doll that walks, talks, wets, cries, and sleeps), what is left but the mechanical manipulation of those machined parts? It is the child who should give life to the doll, not the reverse. Children assume that dolls have human responses—they seem not to realize that it is they who animate the dolls, and breathe into them the qualities they recognize or comprehend and embrace. The rag doll, the cuddly doll, is the one that can be hugged, slept with, retrieved after a few days of neglect, and still remain "intact" after all this.

China dolls, or the old wax dolls, were intimidating and therefore less loved. More admired, perhaps, and highly prized, but less loved. Plastic and composition dolls are not quite so forbidding as china ones, but a child cannot put such a doll beneath her head and sleep comfortably on it. Any time a child is admonished by a mother that she'll "get the doll dirty" or "ruin its hair," that doll does not belong to the child. And few first possessions are more loved or longer remembered than dolls.

Boys are often deprived of the imaginative companionship of dolls because of parental fear that having dolls is too feminine. Cloth animals, especially the familiar teddy bear, seem to provide a rag doll of sorts. Linus's security blanket, made famous by cartoonist Charles Schulz, is just a step removed from the rag doll.

In their third role, dolls as sculpture evolve into a more serious art form. They are rarely produced as sculpture, but rather seem to assume some of the characteristics and qualities of sculpture after they have been completed.

Within this category are some of those dolls produced for adults. They may be serious portraits; they may express a playful or whimsical attitude; they may offer a way of satirizing or caricaturing, or of making comments on human relationships and conditions. These dolls have a simple nature, but they have a presence. Simulacra, such as the waxwork figures found in Madame Tussaud's, or store-window manikins, are characterized by a mock appearance. They are shams, or unreal semblances, pretending to be something which they are not. Dolls have a different nature. They express less of the external similarity and more of the internal characteristics.

One of the striking things about these handmade contemporary dolls is that they are seldom idealized or "pretty." Instead, the doll-forms seem to reflect human beings in the full glory of their vanities, combining lumpy earthiness with human bravado, pride, innocence, and vulgarity. Today's craftsmen seem to be accepting humans as they are, laughing at them and loving them—enjoying their unidealized state. Their weaknesses as humans give them their strength and character as dolls. In these dolls we see ourselves, and perhaps they help us to laugh at ourselves. Without this ability, we are diminished.

Whether dolls are produced as folk art, as toys, or as sculptural forms, the process of creating them is one of personal involvement. The single most delightful thing about these dolls is that each one is completely unique. In the hands of the doll maker, the various materials come to life, and no two dolls will ever be the same. Most doll makers are captivated and intrigued by the way the work itself, once begun, dictates each succeeding step.

One contemporary doll maker, Carol Ann Marsh, in speaking of her own creations (Plate 3), says, "They're so dumpy and perfectly human, and in being so comic give me great pleasure. One never knows what the result will be. They're very organic in that they grow part by part, resulting from the forms previously begun. And lump by lump, you have a person."

Plate 3. "Grandfather" and "Grandmother" by Carol Ann Marsh of LaVerne, Calif. 12 inches and 10 inches high, respectively. Stuffed-fabric dolls with stocking faces; the sculptural effect of the features is accomplished by stitching.

Plate 4. "Marion, the Drunken Bunny Girl" by Carol Anthony of Boston, Mass. Of papier-mâché and fabric. 2½ by 3 feet. (Photo by Becky Young.)

Carol Anthony, whose papier-mâché characters "Russell" and "Walter" as well as "Marion" (Plate 4) are pictured in this book, describes a similar approach. "Sometimes the feeling I see in the Russells and in the Walters [of this world] is best described in rounded 3-D forms," she explains. "The exaggerated feet, the small body, the drape of the pants at the kneecap, the large nose, the big clod spectator shoes can each spell in itself the mood and class of its object without my even starting to paint a face. The character builds itself as I go along."

She continues: "These people are made primarily of sheet mâché, galvanized single-strand wire, newspaper and assorted Salvation Army counter specialties cut down and mâchéd onto the armature. Enamels and wigs, rope, etc., add to the realism and proportion of the statues. They all represent a basic 'Joe' we know or have seen every day on the street corner, at the subway stop, the public commons, the local deli, the Red Sox game at Fen or your local cleaning lady's friend's friend. In other words, they are the color and simplicity *around* us and *in* us all.

"Three-dimensional proportion and humorous exaggeration of the form, plus the excitement and variety of the media, all speak to me graphically and in a total statement that spells it to me more thoroughly than a drawing can. My specialty is humorous statements on the human element—happy, sad, shapeless, wonderful people in their everyday quirks, moods, clothes and predicaments."

Susan Morrison, who makes elaborately pieced dolls (see Color Plates 7 and 8), as well as ornamented forms (Plate 5) comments: "There is never any pattern. Just cutting and sewing and stuffing and embellishing, and then the face goes on and it becomes a doll, a personality. A little humorous, the doll gives you a bit of someone you know, or knew, or would like to know." She adds, "Maybe it's crafts, maybe sculpture. It doesn't have to be either. A doll is a form that is just right to go over and pick up and hold onto."

Regarding her own work (Plate 30, page 59), Nancy Greaver says, "Nothing happens *before* an idea and, if it is a promising one, then the creative process begins—the transmission of an illusive figment of the imagination into something that can be seen and touched."

Because there are so many different approaches to doll making, the dolls in this book are grouped primarily according to their basic structure rather than their purpose. The structural form does not in any way limit the doll's purpose, and the chapter groupings make it easier to describe the various methods of construction. However, there are also overlappings of categories. Certain dolls that are included in a chapter because of specific details of construction could also fit into other chapters.

The whole field of doll making is so vast that it was essential to set some limitations on how much this book could include. The emphasis, therefore, is on homemade dolls constructed of fabric alone or fabric combined with papier-mâché. I find these dolls touching, personal, and intriguing. I prefer seeing a well-loved handmade doll that gives me some insight into its creator to seeing a perfectly preserved china doll resplendent in its original costume. Portraits in doll form vividly describe the nature of the person being depicted. I suppose it is a matter of dolls being as ordinary and everyday as the humans they are intended to describe.

Plate 5. "Doll" by Susan Morrison of Reno, Nev. Stuffed fabric with yarn hair and yarn embroidery. About 9 inches.

2.

SIMPLE DOLLS

Plate 6. A wooden clothespin is shown next to a clothespin doll. The body of the dressed doll is padded and the arms are pipe cleaners. Height 4 inches.

Plate 7. A clothespin is mounted on a stand and a pipe cleaner is wrapped around the body to form arms. Clothespin men by Ruth Law of Claremont, Calif., have dowels inserted for arms. The wood is painted. Height 4 inches.

Simple Dolls

Most children will make dolls of whatever natural materials are available. Few youngsters have never fabricated a figure from a potato, or an acorn, or a walnut. Surely among the first efforts at doll making by many children are dolls of hollyhock blossoms and buds. Toothpicks and the flowers in various stages of blooming are all the materials needed to transform these common plants into girls wearing beautiful dresses (Figure 1). Part of the charm these dolls hold is in their being so ephemeral. They are made to be played with and enjoyed purely within the few hours of their existence. The blossoms are varied in color, and have a beautiful fragrance. Yet it is the child's ingenuity and imagination that turns the hollyhock doll into a vision of elegance.

Perhaps the most touching doll ever collected is one which is displayed in the Museum of Childhood in Edinburgh, Scotland. The doll is made from an old shoe, turned over so that the heel of the shoe suggests a face. Tacks make the eyes, and a mouth is drawn on (Figure 2). It was wrapped in a small blanket and was obviously carried and cradled by a child who nearly wore it out with affection.

A very common homemade doll is one fashioned from a wooden clothespin; the shape of the wood provides a ready-made head and legs, and the doll needs only to be dressed (Plate 6). A face can be drawn on in pencil or with paint. In addition, the clothespin lends itself to many other possibilities. The feet can be sanded off so that the doll will stand more easily, and they can be glued to a base for extra stability. A large button, a poker chip, or a wood disk make suitable stands. For arms, one or more pipe cleaners can be added by wrapping them around the clothespin and gluing them in place, or a dowel can be inserted by drilling a hole through the wood of the clothespin body (Plate 7).

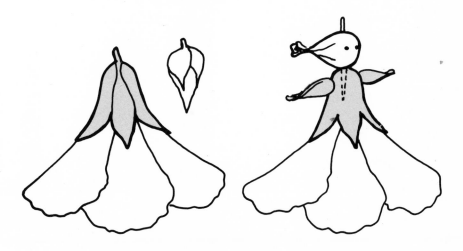

Figure 1. Hollyhock dolls assembled from buds and blossoms are held together with toothpicks. Nearly all children have made floral dolls at some time.

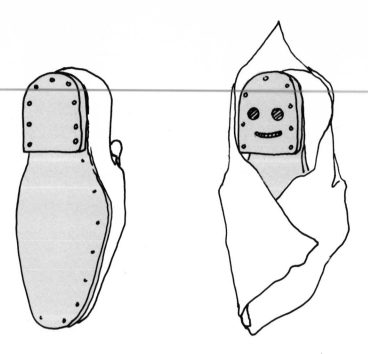

Figure 2. Doll made from an old shoe is on display at the Museum of Childhood in Edinburgh. Along with other dolls made from cast-off material, it is referred to as a "slum doll." Bones were also used for making dolls, with a joint forming the head.

For the beginning doll maker, another popular project is the simplest form of fabric doll (or rag doll, as it is usually called). This is made by forming a wad in the center of a square piece of cloth and tying a string around it to suggest a head. An old handkerchief, a piece of flannel or blanket, or any soft cloth will do as a base fabric. The material is gathered in the center and wound with string or ribbon where the neck would be. Sometimes the head is first stuffed with an additional piece of material. The basic steps, including how to form arms and hands, are shown in Figure 3.

This makes a marvelously simple infant-doll, which is soft and cuddly. Adding a bunting made of another square of material completes the doll. Carrying the form one step further, the lower portion of the doll can be divided for the legs. Such a doll can be made in ten minutes. From this doll form comes the single-shape doll, which allows for a greater detailing of the figure. This will be explored in the next chapter.

Figure 3. The rag doll in its simplest form is made from a square cloth. First a handkerchief or other material is placed over a fingertip with the corners of the cloth hanging down. The end over the finger is arranged in the shape of a head and tied. Sometimes the hollow head is stuffed before being tied. In the next step, hands are suggested by tying the cloth, and features are drawn on. Wrapped in a bunting or blanket, the doll resembles a baby.

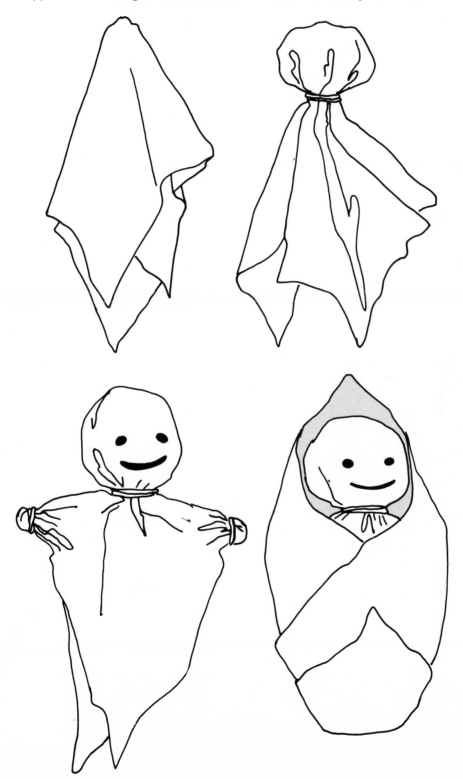

3.

SINGLE-SHAPE DOLLS

Plate 8. The basis of this doll-form is a single shape. Two pieces of fabric are cut to the same shape and sewn together. The form is turned right side out and stuffed. About 16 inches high.

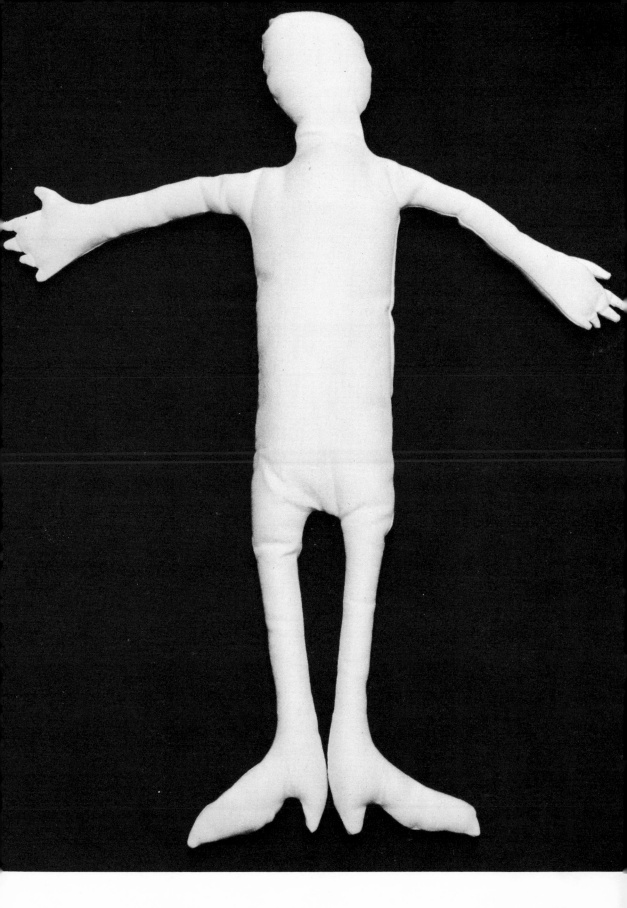

Single-Shape Dolls

Using a single shape as the basis for making a doll is an easy and very versatile method. The doll's head, body, arms and legs are included in one shape. This shape can vary immensely in how much it resembles the human form, ranging from a precise copy to an obscure semblance, according to the doll maker's wishes. In all cases, the outline provides a pattern which is cut out from a double layer of fabric. The edges of the two layers are sewn shut along the entire contour, except for one opening (Figure 4, A). The doll-form is then turned right side out so the seam's edges are inside (Figure 4, B), and rags, batting or other soft material is pushed through the opening in the seam. When the form is adequately stuffed, the opening in the seam is slip-stitched closed.

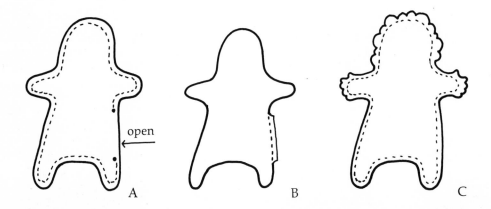

Figure 4. The two pieces of material cut from a single pattern are placed together as shown in A and sewn (dashed lines). An opening must be left at one side. Drawing B shows the doll after it has been turned. At this point it is stuffed; then the opening is slip-stitched shut. Drawing C shows the procedure if felt is used. In that case, the doll is stuffed as it is stitched, and it need not be turned.

Figure 5. These simple variations of the single-shape doll offer animation to the form.

If felt is used, the doll can be stitched from the outside in stages as you alternately stitch and stuff the form until it is complete (Figure 4,C). This eliminates the need to turn the material once it is sewn. (See doll in Plate 9.)

Features may be drawn on the doll with marking pens or paints, or they can be appliquéd or embroidered. Animation can be partially achieved through the shaping of the body posture, arms and legs, as in Figure 5.

Plate 8 shows the basic form of a two-piece doll derived from a single shape. The two pieces of material were cut according to the desired shape and sewn. The resulting form was turned and stuffed so that it is now ready to have features added, hair sewn on, and clothing made. Though in some cases it may be best to sew the face on first, while the material is flat, it is generally easier to determine the placement of eyes and other facial details after the head is stuffed. This also gives you a form to hold onto as you sew, and knots may be concealed where they will later be covered by hair or by appliqué.

A completed doll with appliquéd features, "Mermaid" (Plate 9) was machine sewn using two identical felt shapes. The contour of the form gives it an animated quality. Scales and features were added with hand-stitching. This is a doll which can easily be made in an hour.

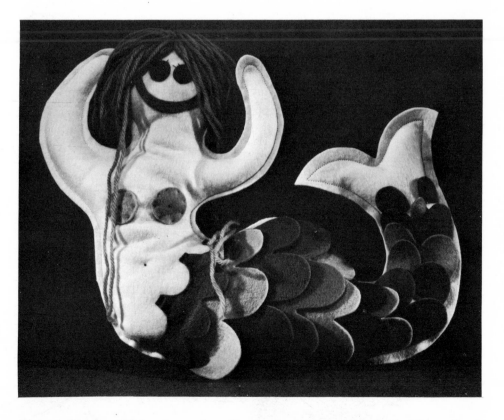

Plate 9. "Mermaid" by the author. Single-shape doll of felt with felt appliqué. Length is 15 inches. When felt is used, the stitching may be done on the outside of the form and the shape does not then need to be turned.

The figure in Plate 10 is also a completed single-shape doll. It was cut double from cotton fabric, which was sewn, turned, and stuffed. The same doll, shown with a dress, is seen in Plate 11.

Another single-shape doll, the marvelously detailed "Viking" (Plate 12) by Bucky King, is a simple form but achieves complexity through the treatment of the surface in textures, patterns and suggestions of ornamental detail.

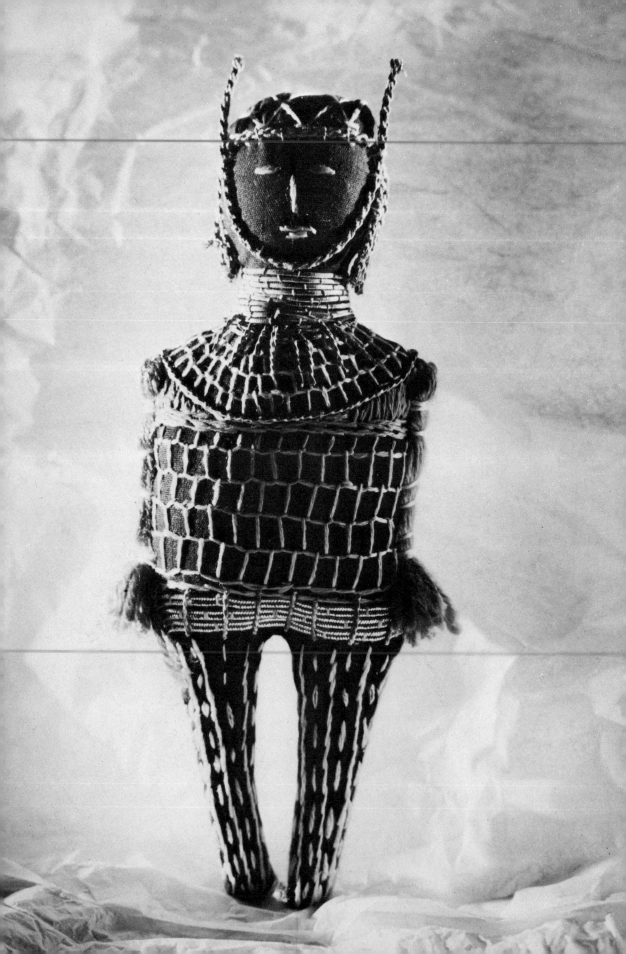

Several examples by Lenore Davis illustrate how you can take full advantage of the single shape to create something that surpasses the limitations of a simple doll-form. In her "Group of Five" (Plate 13), she artistically explores the expansive possibilities of the composite-body doll. Her keen perception startles us into new realizations about humans and the relationships between them.

Plate 13. "Group of Five" by Lenore Davis of Buffalo, New York. Standing profile of five persons incorporated in a single shape. Made of brown velveteen, the noses are sculptured by stitching. Folds in the material appear at necklines and thighs. 15 inches by 22 inches. (Photo by Lenore Davis.)

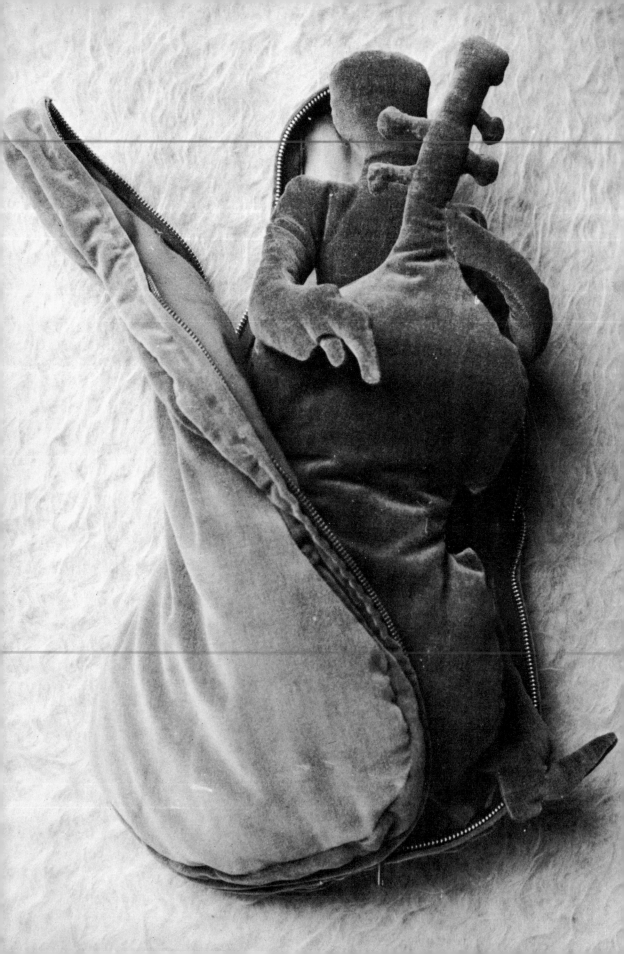

"Case, Bass, Man" (Plate 14), another of her delightful works, deals with the relationship between a man and two inanimate objects. "Brown Angel" (Plate 15) demonstrates her ability to animate the figure with only slight body movement, made possible by the way in which she has stitched joints across the arms and the legs.

The jointed, single-shape doll is begun in the same fashion as the unjointed type, but sections are sewn off as soon as they are stuffed, providing an unstuffed line that allows the fabric to bend or turn easily at these joints. The sections are stuffed and sewn off in order, starting with the farthest portions of the limbs and working toward the body and the head. (See Figure 6.)

Figure 6. Sewing off joints as you stuff the single shape makes it possible to bend the arms and legs at the stitched lines.

Plate 15. "Brown Angel" by Lenore Davis is single-shaped with wings added and joints stitched in the brown velveteen. The face is appliquéd to the head and the features are dye-painted. Unspun wool hair. 16 inches high. (Photo by Lenore Davis.)

Plate 16. Fabric doll from a single shape has a joint of stitching at the legs. From the collection of Helen Trimble. 10 inches high.

Depending upon the amount of stuffing, the doll can be floppy and cuddly, or fairly stiff and rigid. Plate 16 shows a tightly stuffed, single-shape doll in which just one seam gives the legs potential movement. This sewing-off method is carried a step further in the example of a loosely stuffed doll (Plate 17) which has two joints for each arm and three for each leg. This makes it possible to put the doll into a number of various positions.

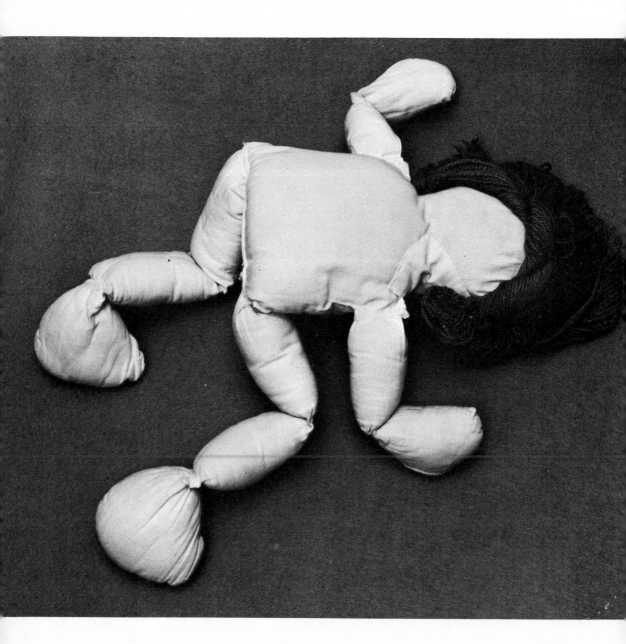

Plate 17. Rag doll by Betsy O'Hara has stitched arm and leg joints on attached limbs.

Plate 18. "Five Girl Chorus Line" by Lenore Davis is a single shape with stitched joints for animation. Of dye-painted velveteen, the chorus girls have pink and orange costumes and red-orange unspun wool hair. 18 inches by 21 inches. (Photo by Lenore Davis.)

"Five Girl Chorus Line" (Plate 18) beautifully exemplifies the stitching technique used to make joints on the limbs of single-shape dolls and thus animate or give movement to the arms and legs, in this case animating the five dancing figures.

As you can see, the sewing-off of joints in single-shape dolls is the basis for jointed dolls made of more than one shape. (The rag doll in Plate 17 has separate limbs joined to the head-and-body-form.) The joining of various parts to form a doll requires techniques to be discussed in the next chapter.

4.

JOINTED DOLLS

Plate 19. Antique fabric doll made in 1870 has limbs attached separately, showing simple jointing. From the collection of Helen Trimble. Height 8 inches.

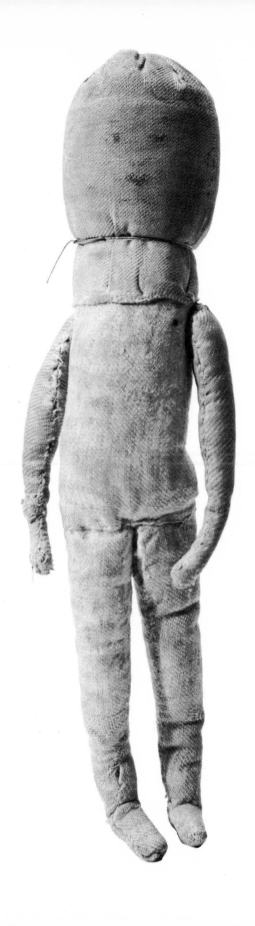

Jointed Dolls

In general, dolls that are termed "jointed" are made of more than one shape; the different parts are made separately and then added on. Usually the head and limbs are added to a body form. Sometimes the head and neck are formed with the body and, besides separate limbs, other parts—such as a nose, ears, and hands—are added later. The separate pieces are completely sewn, turned and stuffed before being joined. It is easiest to handle the joining if the body is stuffed first so that there is a firm base or form to which other parts can be added.

The child's doll in Plate 19 has simple jointing and is about one hundred years old. The fabric is nearly threadbare, and the doll was obviously handled and loved and saved. This mere suggestion of the form is all that is demanded in a child's toy. It is sewn together with an overcast stitch (whipstitch).

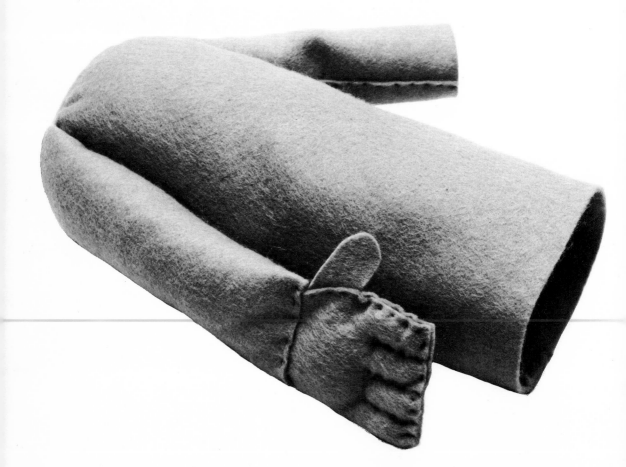

Plate 20. Basic cylinder forms for doll construction were made in felt by the author. The seams are hand-sewn with a running stitch. Cylindrical arm is flattened at shoulder joint and at wrist to simplify attaching the parts, which are stuffed before being joined. Height 9 inches.

Figure 7. Dolls can be assembled from a series of cylinder forms. Long cylinders can be used for bodies, arms, and legs; short sections (drum shapes) are usable as heads.

A simple means of joining parts of a doll is shown in Plate 20. This body is made from felt, and the structure consists of a series of cylindrical forms. The arms are cylinders attached to a body of the same basic form. The upper portion of the body was stuffed before the arms were added. The hand shown was sewn separately and lightly stuffed.

Dolls can be made by joining these cylinders in various ways. Figure 7 suggests some of these. If the arms and legs are flattened at one end, attaching them to the body is greatly simplified. Note that the heads in Figure 7 are made from a truncated cylinder resulting in a drum shape. "Lazy Lily" (Plate 21) has such a head, with the arms, legs and body formed from simple two-piece structures.

A charming doll by Kathy Fukami Glascock shows a back view of the arm sewn separately to the body (Plate 22). In this case, the fabric used for the dress was sewn to each body part before they were connected. The hair is carefully stitched on the cloth head.

Among the most appealing jointed dolls for children are those dolls made by Joyce Weiss. The facial expressions are direct and joyous (Plates 23 and 24). None has the simpering smile found on so many "pretty" manufactured dolls. Their softness and the floppiness of their limbs make it difficult to look at these dolls without reaching out to pick them up. They are constructed with the head and body cut from a single shape and with the arms and legs added.

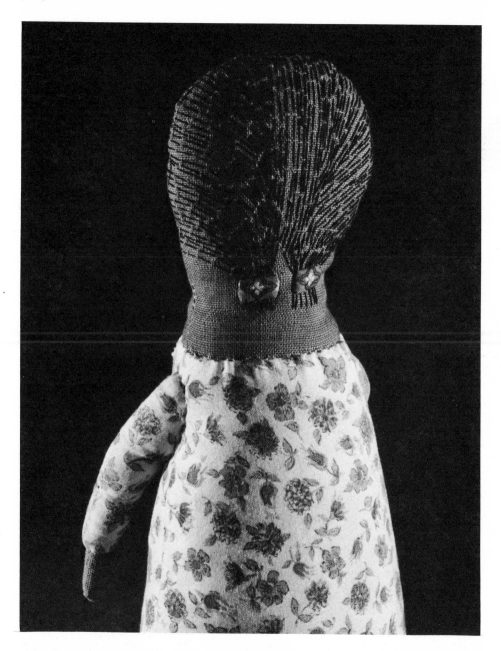

The "Starlet" doll (Plate 25) was put together by completing one stage at a time. The head was stuffed and tied; then the body was stuffed. The lower portion of the body was split to make the legs, which were then sewn. Arms were stitched and stuffed, then joined to the body. All the forms were made from a stocking of white nylon, giving a somewhat sickly pallor to this sunbathing would-be goddess.

Plate 23. "Dolls" by Joyce Weiss of Palos Verdes Estates, Calif. Arms and legs were added to each single-shape head and body. Appliquéd faces and yarn hair complete the happy figures. Height 15 inches, 25 inches.

Plate 24. "Doll" by Joyce Weiss. Felt features are appliquéd on the fabric head. Body is stuffed with kapok.

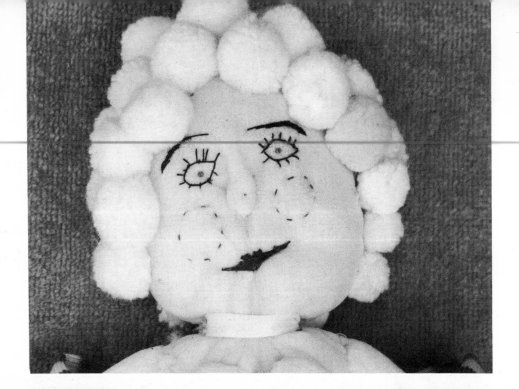

Plate 25. "Starlet" by the author. A white nylon stocking provides the head, body and legs of this sunbather. Arms are added. Details are embroidered and the hair is made of ball fringe. Facial features are formed by stitching both the cloth and the stuffing together.

Plate 26. Doll from Appalachia. Stuffed cotton fabric. The nose and the feet are formed separately and sewn on. Height 17 inches.

A typical Appalachian doll, found in the Southeastern part of the country, uses piecing to add details (Plate 26). The feet are not an extension of the fabric used on the legs, but rather are separate forms. The nose, too, is added. It is a "button" form and gives a greater dimension to the otherwise nearly flat face.

"Sister" (Plate 27) by Pauline Thompson is a jointed doll with stuffed arms and legs. The head and body were combined in a single form. The materials used on the doll were selected to a great degree for the interplay of textures rather than for realism in depiction of an ornately dressed lady.

Plate 27. "Sister" by Pauline Thompson of Los Angeles. Jointed arms and legs are of fabric. The costume of old beads, lace, feathers, fur and fabric display a pleasure in the use of textures.

1. *"Beach Honey" by Carol Anthony. Of papier-mâché, about 15 inches high, this Honey, circa 1890, is one of a series of "Beach Walkers." (Photo by Bob Lovering.)*

2. "Doll" by Gloria McNutt. Stuffed cotton fabric in bright colors with felt appliqué makes this a delightfully direct and open-faced doll. Height 12 inches. (Photo by Gloria McNutt.)

3. "Two Girls" by Joyce Weiss. These fabric dolls with felt appliqué features have floppy, movable limbs and are 15 inches high.

4. "Flat Pat" by the author. Dolls are silk-screened on felt, then cut and sewn. Height 11 inches.

5. "Astronaut and Martians" by Penelope Greeven, from drawings by her eight-year-old son Chris. Figures drawn in colored marking pens were transferred to equally bright felts. Average size about 9 inches.

6. "Angel" by Susan Morrison. Elaborate yarn hairdo and gold trim on the costume set off the delicate little face of this pillow doll. Rectangle is 17 inches long.

7. "Circus Lady" by Susan Morrison. A fat, velvet hippo is placed within nibbling distance of the performer's arm and flowers. Both forms are carefully pieced and then stuffed. Height 32 inches.

8. "Weight Lifter" by Susan Morrison. Bold colors of the appliquéd costume and detailed embroidery are combined to complete the character of this pieced doll. Height 35 inches.

9. "Lady Astride a Ram" by Susan Morrison. Beautifully structured ram holds the austere-looking lady whose outfit is richly embroidered but prim and precise. Height 25 inches.

10. "Nickolos and Nastasha" by Nita Bartelmes. Finger puppets, made from felt, have colorful embroidered details. About 5 inches.

11. "Doll" from Appalachia. The feet are constructed separately and added to the sturdy, stuffed-fabric figure. Height 17 inches.

12. "Girl" by the author. Felt doll is cut from a simple arch shape. Arms are appliquéd and legs inserted in seam at bottom edge. Overall height 18 inches.

13. "Rapunzel" by the author. Finger puppet is made of felt, and hair is raveled gold-colored brocade. Height 5 inches.

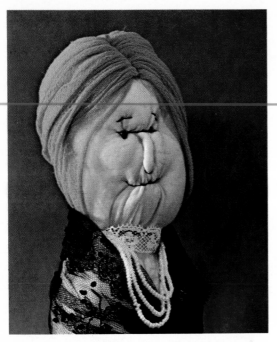

14. *"Chaperone" by the author. Nylon stocking is filled with Dacron batting, then stitched to form the features. Doll is 14 inches tall.*

15. *"Matador" by Emelia Casada. The figure is elaborately costumed in velour and brocade. The stocking face is stitched to give a sculptural effect to nose and eyes. Doll is 32 inches tall.*

16. *"Grandmother" by Carol Ann Marsh. A stocking-face portrait doll with features formed by stitching. Height 10 inches.*

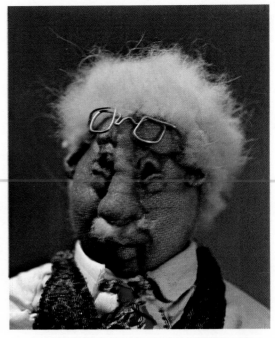

17. *"Grandfather" by Carol Ann Marsh. Wire eyeglasses add to the portrait of the benevolent-looking gentleman. Hair is of fur.*

The incredible creations of Susan Morrison combine a variety of joining techniques. The arms of her "Weight Lifter" (Plate 28) are cut in one piece with the body, while the head and legs are sewn separately and added. Susan uses many different textures in very complex combinations, choosing whatever materials she feels will accomplish her desired effect. Such objects as bells, beads, and yarns provide extra decorative touches to the various fabrics. Appliqué, embroidery and three-dimensional construction are all things which she handles with ease. The Hippo, nestled above "Circus Lady" (Plate 29) is a marvelous assembly of velour forms, while the lady herself is a humorous amalgamation of a satin-costumed body, net-stockinged legs, and an undersized yarn-covered head.

Plate 28. "The Weight Lifter" by Susan Morrison. This magnificent strong man, with barbell and bird, results from intricate piecing, detailed embroidery and a keen eye for the absurd. Height 35 inches.

A completely different approach is presented in the pieced doll (Plate 30) by Nancy Greaver. Such construction allows a more accurate three-dimensional shaping in the face and neck, and many dolls produced from patterns make use of it. Patience is required to figure out this piecing, but trial and error will lead you to these forms. Anyone who understands clothing construction and tailoring can undoubtedly manage this approach easily. The seams that show in the photograph of Nancy's doll serve to describe how she achieved the form. The decorative details were added with embroidery and couching. Small wooden beads are threaded in the doll's yarn hair, where—in keeping with the doll's lyrical quality—a small bird rests.

Describing her work method, Nancy Greaver says, "I nearly always try to get the idea on paper first, into some sort of visual form. Then I work out a pattern using inexpensive muslin, and pursue a course of trial and error until I feel the proportions are right and the design is carrying out my original conception. The fabric chosen for the finished doll is then cut and sewn and stuffed with kapok."

Plate 30. "Puff" by Nancy Greaver of Albuquerque, N. Mex. A well-constructed and tightly padded doll of Mexican cotton. Yarn is used for the hair and is couched to the fabric for costume detail. Height 12 inches.

In speaking of her motivation, she adds, "Except that I want to and must, I can think of no other reason to make dolls. Happiness is creating, so I keep at it. I feel fortunate to accomplish even one idea in ten, but I think the excitement engendered in the pursuit of that one idea is the 'why' of it."

Plate 31. "Teen-agers" by M. Nelson Hooton of Albuquerque, N. Mex. Figures are formed by skillful seaming and stuffing. Carefully detailed embroidery defines the features of these gangly teen-agers. Height about 42 inches.

Plate 32. "Dancing Couple" by Lenore Davis. Double figure in unbleached muslin is made from a single shape except for added arms that create further unity. Faces are machine-embroidered; hair is unspun wool. Height 12 inches. (Photo by Lenore Davis.)

Nancy's approach is more systematic and studied than that used by some doll makers who say their dolls "grow," or take form, as they work on them. No one way of working can be said to be better than another. The important thing is to find the ways that work best for you.

In "Teen-agers" (Plate 31), M. Nelson Hooton employs a variety of piecing and forming methods to obtain a superb measure of dimension. The dolls, nearly 4 feet tall, have carefully sewn and stuffed ears, fingers, and noses. Their large scale makes it possible to clothe them in some ready-made goods (often modified by hand-sewing) as well as in homemade articles. Much of the dolls' charm is in their embroidered faces, full of detail and rich color. They are such good-humored, loving spoofs that most teen-agers would enjoy being caricatured in this way.

The two jointed figures by Lenore Davis are entirely different in execution than the "Teen-agers." Her work "Dancing Couple" (Plate 32) adds arms that are separate from the body forms, but which serve to further join one figure with another. She opens up possibilities in doll making that have seldom been explored. Her work is unique for the way in which she uses the fabric to suggest relationships between people while it also suggests their forms.

5.

ARCH-SHAPED DOLLS

Plate 33. "Girls" by the author. Simple arch shapes provide the basic form for these dolls. Unstuffed arch shapes are added for arms and feet. Iron-on tape is used for features and decorative edgings provide details of clothing. Height ranges from 6 to 10 inches.

Arch-Shaped Dolls

The arch-shaped doll is basically a single-shape doll but it can be considered a jointed doll whenever arms and legs are added separately to the simple arch shape. Since this manner of construction is so flexible and lends itself to such a wide range of variations, it has been placed in a separate category. Some examples of this approach to doll making are included in Color Plates 4 and 12.

Within the arch-shaped form you can define the head, the features, and the clothing—and often arms and legs as well—by sewing or gluing other materials to the sewn and stuffed forms. If arms and legs are added so that they extend from the form, you can make these extensions from unstuffed arch shapes such as those in Plate 33. Each doll in the photograph has arms added and two have feet. The features are all made of iron-on mending tape, cut to shape and pressed on; ready-made edgings and fringes are sewn on to suggest clothing.

The basic body-form is shown in Figure 8. The extensions (arms and legs, or hands and feet) are finished, sewn, and turned. They are inserted in the seam line of the body-form before it is sewn and turned. Figures 9 and 10 suggest other possibilities using the confines of this arch form. Arms, legs, hands, and feet do not have to be limited to the arch shape and they can be defined within the arch as well as added to it. They do not even have to be added at all (Plate 34).

Figure 8. The arch shape is cut double, with hands and feet made separately and inserted in the seam. An opening must be left so that the doll can be turned and stuffed. The last drawing shows the doll turned right side out, with hands and feet extended.

Figure 9. Using the basic arch shape for body and head, arms and hands may also be kept within the arch and only legs need to be added.

Figure 10. Other possibilities for dolls within the limitations of the simple arch shape are shown here.

Using the same arch shape but adding limbs and details entirely within the simple form is a technique exemplified by Mary Isenberg's dolls (Plates 35 and 36). Here embroidery and cloth appliqué are effectively combined to provide all the details.

Plate 34. "Red Riding Hood" by the author has features of iron-on tape. Two squares of fabric, red and pink, are sewn together, turned, and pressed to suggest the cape. Height of doll is 9 inches.

Plate 35. "Jeanine, the Can-Can Dancer" by Mary Isenberg. Forms indicated by running-stitch embroidery and by appliqué on a cotton base. Height 10 inches.

Plate 36. "Mother and Baby" by Mary Isenberg of Turlock, Calif. Simple arch-shaped dolls with decorative running-stitch embroidery to define features. Hands are appliquéd within the arch. Height 11 inches.

You can combine the technique of adding limbs that extend from the body-form with that of adding limbs which stay within the arch shape. Plate 37 shows a felt doll with the legs cut from a single layer of material and added by inserting them at the bottom of the lightly stuffed body-form. An additional layer of felt was sewn to the basic form to suggest the dress. Arms overlap this, so that four to five layers of felt are stacked in some areas. This adds weight to the felt doll and gives it a bit more rigidity.

The merest suggestion of arms and legs can also be made with small knob-like protrusions. Three dolls by Joan Orme use this simple form. The arms are cut and stuffed with the body, and the feet are made separately and attached (Plates 38, 39, and 40). Heavy textures, patterned fabrics and appliqué enrich the forms.

Plate 37. "Doll" by the author. Running stitch and French knots are used for appliquéd arms, features and costume. Felt legs and feet are added to the arch shape.

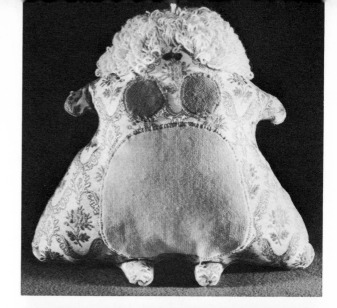

Plate 38. "Marie Antoinette" by Joan Orme of Palos Verdes Estates, Calif. Arch shape with extended arms and added feet. Stuffed brocade and velour, yarn-stitched hair. Height about 12 inches.

Plate 39. "Hester" by Joan Orme. Machine-appliquéd flowers embellish the simple form of this doll. Height 11 inches.

Plate 40. "Lulu" by Joan Orme. Appliquéd velour with yarn-stitched hair.

Plate 41. "Doll" by Sandie Piper of Fresno, Calif. The figure is hand-sewn felt, with the decorative details glued into place.

Plate 42. "Lady" by Susan Morrison. Stuffed-fabric doll with looped yarn hair. Details in felt appliqué combined with yarns couched to the fabric. Height 20 inches.

Plate 43. "People Watchers" by the author. Flat dolls of various geometric shapes are suspended by threads. Each is made from two pieces of fabric, sewn and turned but not stuffed. Height 6 to 10 inches.

Ornamenting the form is a highly creative work in itself. Both Susan Morrison and Sandie Piper make elaborate use of yarns. The basic construction of the very decorative doll by Sandie Piper is stuffed felt (Plate 41). Sandie then glued yarn to the felt in what she terms a "wet embroidery." Susan Morrison's fabric doll has couched-yarn embroidery along with very delicate felt appliqué, all hand-stitched (Plate 42).

Other geometric forms can be combined with the arch shape, as the unstuffed dolls in Plate 43 illustrate. These dolls are flat pieces of fabric, with faces on both sides. They are hung from threads, and the legs are joined by threads. Cotton broadcloth, felt, and percale were used. The eyes are suggested with ready-made edgings, and the mouths are embroidered.

Used separately, the triangle provides the basic form for Gloria McNutt's delightful appliqué doll shown in Color Plate 2. Triangular, rectangular, or circular forms lend themselves very readily to the construction of pillow dolls, which are chunkier versions of the arch-shaped doll.

6.

PILLOW DOLLS

Plate 44. "Dude" by the author. A pillow, 13 inches by 15 inches, forms the base for this doll. The head, in the shape of a drum, is stitched to the top. Hands and feet are inserted in the seams at the edges of the pillow covering.

Pillow Dolls

A pillow doll is simply a doll which takes its basic form from a large, blocky shape. You can utilize a real pillow and add to it, or you can stuff a doll in such a way that it becomes like a pillow.

Pillow dolls can be functional. A group of them on a sofa makes an amusing and delightful collection. For the child, a pillow doll is a plaything that can also be tucked under the head. Or it can, of course, be used in a magnificent pillow fight in which the "people" go flying through the air.

Any pillow which you already have will do for a start. If you are using a bed pillow and find that it is too soft or too loosely stuffed, tuck in one end and slip-stitch or topstitch it closed. This will make the pillow firmer and fuller, and easier to handle. A pillowcase can be appliquéd, with the arms and legs extending from the case. This method would allow easy removal for cleaning. The arms and legs extending from the pillowcase should each be made of two pieces of fabric, sewn and turned. Stuffing them would make them too heavy in terms of the weight of the pillowcase.

A second way of working with the bed pillow is to make arms and legs, stuff them, and attach them to the pillow itself. The doll's costume could then be sewn to the pillowcase. By cutting holes in the case for the arms and legs to go through, you can slip the costume onto the doll. Or you can sew material directly to the pillow itself, making the decoration non-removable and the pillow non-washable but resulting in a more doll-like creation. Some suggestions for pillow dolls are given in Figure 11.

Figure 11. A bed pillow can be used for the head and body of a doll, with arms, legs and details added.

74

Plate 45. "Three-Cornered Ladies" by Joyce Aiken of Fresno, Calif. Each doll is a triangular pillow with face and hands appliquéd and hair added.

Smaller sofa pillows are even easier to adapt as pillow dolls. The pillow is used to suggest the major body form; hands and feet—and sometimes the head—are added. The doll in Plate 44 is made from a pillow with the body appliquéd in felt. Hands and shoes are each double layers of felt topstitched together. The head is made and stuffed separately, and then slip-stitched to the top of the pillow, which is 13 inches by 15 inches. The face is detailed with felt appliqué and embroidery.

The pillow does not have to be rectangular. Each of the dolls in the collection by Joyce Aiken uses a triangle to form the entire body (Plate 45). The arms, or the hands, and the face are sewn onto the front surface, using a different color of felt to set them apart from the body. Like the arch and the rectangle, the triangle offers an opportunity for experimentation within a simple form (Figure 12).

Figure 12. The triangular pillow suggests figures that fit into that shape.

Figure 13. Rectangular pillows used horizontally have heads made separately and added.

Each geometric shape has its own potentials for doll making. A long, narrow pillow is good to work with because the shape suggests exaggerations and variations of the figure. This shape can be used horizontally (Figure 13) or vertically (Figure 14). The vertical form is more apt to include the head within the pillow form, while the head is usually added to the horizontal form. The arms and legs are stuffed and stitched to the body.

The advantage in starting off with a ready-made pillow is that much of the work is already completed for you. You need only make small additions to the primary pillow-form. If you prefer starting from scratch and stuffing a doll to resemble a pillow, you still have the advantage of the simplified form.

Figure 14. Used vertically, rectangular pillows are more apt to include the head.

Plate 46. "Angel" by Susan Morrison. The heavily stuffed, blocky form of this doll suggests its use as a pillow. Length 17 inches.

"Angel" (Plate 46), Susan Morrison's delightfully worldly though tinsel-covered creation, has a blocky form that puts it in the category of a pillow doll. The doll does have wings, which heighten its aspirations towards the angelic, but they do not show in the front view. Green hair, and rich decorative detail in gold trim and braid add complexity to the simple form (see Color Plate 6).

Several of the arch-shaped dolls in the preceding chapter can also be considered pillow dolls. For the beginner, a pillow doll offers an excellent first project. With much of the basic form complete it is possible to concentrate on those details which are the most fun in doll making—the animation of the figure, the ornamentation of the costume and the detailing of features.

7.

TRANSFERRING CHILDREN'S IDEAS INTO DOLLS

Plate 47. "Isme" by Penelope Greeven, adapted from a cardboard doll made by her son Brett. The figure is cut from bright yellow-and-orange striped fabric. Height about 16 inches.

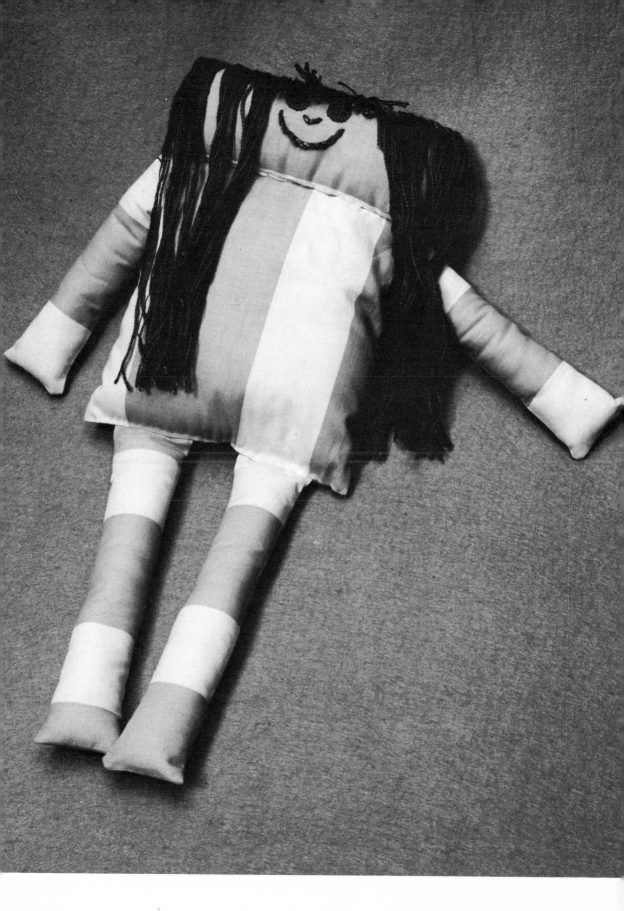

Transferring Children's Ideas into Dolls

Just as pillow dolls can serve a dual purpose by giving their creators an opportunity for experimentation and at the same time giving children pleasure as playthings, making dolls expressly for children is also rewarding. One of the best sources of ideas for children's dolls is the children themselves. They will often make dolls on their own, using whatever materials they find at hand. Their inventiveness should not be overlooked as inspiration for your own doll making.

Using fabric, Penelope Greeven re-created a cardboard doll made by her son Brett when he was five. Brett constructed the original doll from a shirt box. He tore the sides off and used the two small ends for arms and the two long ones for legs. These were stapled into place. Yarn hair was stapled on, and a face was added. Figure 15 shows how he assembled the doll. From this cardboard figure, Mrs. Greeven made her version of the doll (Plate 47). Stuffed fabric was substituted for the paper, but construction was similar.

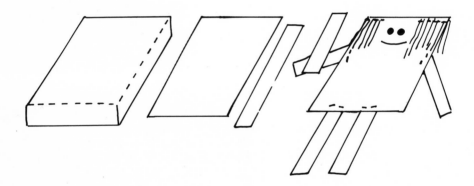

Figure 15. A five-year-old took a cardboard shirt box apart and reassembled the pieces to form a simple figure. Arms, legs, and hair are stapled in place.

The doll Brett made is typical of what most children, allowed to exercise their imagination and given the use of materials and tools, will produce. When my daughter was four, she made a doll for herself of the most likely (and most liked) material at hand—masking tape (Plate 48). Marking pens were used to draw the face, but it wore away with handling. She always took far more interest in making dolls than in playing with them.

Children are open to possibilities which most adults no longer see. So take time to look at your children's creations, and be inspired by them. The relationship during those early years provides a chance to share experiences, and the mother who doesn't learn as much from her child as the child learns from her may be missing one of the most exciting aspects of child-rearing.

Plate 48. "Man" by Lizabeth Laury at age four. Masking tape is wrapped, wadded and folded to form this doll. Most children will make similar dolls from whatever materials they have at hand. Height 7 inches.

Plate 49. "Me," drawn by Alison Law at age six, was transferred to felt and machine-sewn by her mother. Height 16 inches.

Most children readily draw self-portraits and are delighted with the idea of seeing dolls of themselves. One approach is to simply transfer the child's self-portrait into a doll form (Plate 49). Another is for you to have the child lie down on a large piece of wrapping paper so you can trace all around him and use the outline as a pattern. Allowing extra for seams, cut the shape from doubled fabric. Sew, turn and stuff the form. Draw features on the doll and add hair. Though the doll will end up being somewhat smaller than life size because of the material taken up in the stuffing, it can still be dressed in the child's own clothes. With experience you may prefer to make an allowance for the material used up by the curvatures of the stuffed form.

Mothers and teachers can fashion dolls based on children's sketches, drawings, paintings or cut-paper work (Plates 50 and 51). The child can even draw directly on fabric with fabric markers; then the material can be cut around the outline of the figure, and sewn.

Drawing the doll directly on the fabric and coloring it in a batik process is a bit more complex, but worth the effort. The dyeing method is similar to a regular batik process, but substitutes materials which children can easily handle and which are less expensive.

First, a piece of old sheeting is placed on a large rectangle of cardboard and attached with masking tape, as in Figure 16, A. Then the child draws the doll on the sheeting with water-soluble markers or permanent laundry markers. Permanent color is preferable, though either can be used.

When the drawing is finished, undo one side of the tape. Bend the cardboard so that it forms a cradle, lifting the sheeting above the cardboard (Figure 16, B). Replace the tape to keep the sheeting in that position. Heat paraffin, adding beeswax if it is available. The beeswax mixture is less brittle, when cooled, than the all-paraffin coating, which tends to crack. Since the function of the wax is to cover the areas already drawn and protect them from the dye, you do not want it to crack. In some batiks, cracking is desirable, as it forms a network of dye pattern over the fabric.

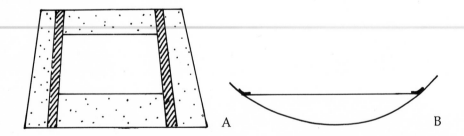

Figure 16. To use a simple batik process, attach a piece of fabric to a sheet of cardboard with two strips of masking tape, as in A. Make a marking-pen drawing of the doll on the fabric and when it is complete untape one side of the fabric. Bend the cardboard into a cradle as shown, and retape the cloth. A side view of this is shown in B. Now when the wax is applied it will not stick to the cardboard.

Plate 50. "Astronaut and Martians" by Chris Greeven, age eight, and his mother. Original drawings, done with marking pens, were transferred to felt. These dolls combine hand-sewing with machine-stitching. Height 6 to 8 inches.

Use caution in heating the wax, which is flammable. Placing a container of wax in a pan of water is a safe way to heat it. Do not heat wax over a direct flame or burner. Penelope Greeven suggests heating the wax in an old electric coffee-pot, as it allows you to control the temperature and not exceed the melting point.

With a brush, paint melted wax over every area drawn in with colored marker. Overlap each brushstroke of wax slightly to seal in the drawing. If the marker lines are not completely covered with wax, any water-soluble color may run when the wet dye is put on.

With the sheeting still attached to the cardboard, let the child brush dye over the entire surface. Food coloring, while not permanent, is bright and usually available. For permanence, use one of the commonly available liquid dyes. Blot the sheeting with paper towels, to get rid of excess moisture, and remove it from the cardboard. Hang the fabric to dry.

Plate 51. "Boy Riding His Kangaroo" was drawn by Chris Greeven and adapted by his mother. Bright-colored felts were hand-sewn and stuffed. Height 9 inches.

Plate 52. "Batik Doll" by Chris Greeven. The doll is drawn on fabric with marking pen; then the drawn areas are covered with wax. Remaining portions of doll are colored by dyeing the fabric before cutting and sewing the shape. Height 10 inches.

When dry, place the waxed and dyed cloth between clean sheets of shelf paper, paper towels, or butcher's paper. (Ink rubs off, so avoid newsprint.) Iron out the wax using a medium heat setting. Melted wax is absorbed by the paper so, as you iron, the papers must be changed often.

Cut out the shape of the doll, allowing material for seams. Cut another piece from that same pattern, using a solid color or a printed fabric for the back. Sew the two pieces together inside out, turn and stuff.

Food colors can be purchased by the pint or quart, or even the gallon if you are going to use it for groups. Penelope Greeven, whose son painted the batik doll in Plate 52, had an entire class of fifth graders complete the batik process in a morning. She diluted colors to make them go farther, and they retained most of their brilliance. Unless colorfast markers and dye are used, these dolls will not be washable.

Children's drawings are a great source for figures. For dolls they can be enlarged if necessary, and sometimes they will need to be adapted. Generally, selecting simple drawings will assure a simply made doll. Figure 17 shows some work by a six-year-old which could easily be turned into dolls.

Figure 17. Children's drawings are usually simple and blocky and can readily be adapted as fabric dolls.

8.

FACES & HAIR

Plate 53. "Nurse" by the author. A little larger than life size, the face has features of stuffed-fabric appliqué. The hair is made from brown broadcloth and stuffed.

Faces and Hair

It is no coincidence that when children draw a picture of themselves or of the people around them they place the most emphasis on the face and its features, with the body often being just a stick figure. To children as well as adults the face is the most revealing aspect of a person. In our day-to-day dealings with other people, we interpret from gestures, posture, tone of voice, and words. But no single factor is more important to us than the *look*—what we read on a person's face.

The unguarded face offers us an open book through which we may read behavior, thought, or attitude. Reacting to what we see, we have certain feelings about individual faces and facial expressions. The same expressions when seen on dolls' faces evoke related feelings in us, and it is this evocation that gives character and substance to the dolls.

The face is a coherent display of marvelously efficient sensory organs, each of which provides the doll maker with unlimited opportunities for portraying expression. The eyes on a doll's face can communicate the doll's character to us because in life eyes are used to transmit feelings as well as to take in information. In fact, we sometimes turn away from a person's gaze because he reveals more than we can comfortably accept. And, at the other extreme, we seem utterly without privacy when a person looks straight into our eyes. Certainly it is difficult not to betray embarrassment, or guilt, or amusement when another person looks within us through our eyes. But a doll's eyes function solely to convey an expression. With dolls, we are free to look or search for what is being revealed, knowing that we are not being searched in turn.

The mouth is as significant as the eyes in expression. The set of the lips, a pinched mouth or an open one, protruding teeth—all these things tend to be read as indicative of personality. Of all the features, certainly the nose is the most often ridiculed. Certain sizes, shapes and colors seem within acceptable limits. Beyond those limits, the proportions verge on the absurd, and become humorous or grotesque. This is also true of the ears.

Other parts of the face also help form character. Cheeks may be full and colorful in youth, hollowed and pale in age. The chin may suggest a reticent or aggressive nature. Eyebrows play an important descriptive role. Brows high above the eyes tend to produce a wide-eyed look, innocent and babylike. As the brows become heavier, lower, and closer together, they assume a complexity of characteristics. Many of these examples suggest stereotyped responses to the face because the features are often used to categorize people. But features also describe the uniqueness of the individual.

In doll making, the features may be applied in many different ways. In other chapters, we have seen the use of iron-on tape, marking pens, appliqué and embroidery. Here we see some examples of stuffed features added to the face and get a close-up look at how the details of the face and the hair combine to give the doll its character.

"Nurse" (Plate 53) utilizes stuffed-fabric appliqué for the eyebrows, eyelids, cheeks, lips, and chin. Small bits of Dacron batting are used for this. The nose is pleated at the bottom so that it stands out about an inch from the face. Because the doll is slightly larger than life size, the details, such as eyelids, can be appliquéd easily. On smaller faces, it would be harder to appliqué such tiny shapes. The hair is sewn of cotton broadcloth and stuffed. Figure 18 shows how this is done.

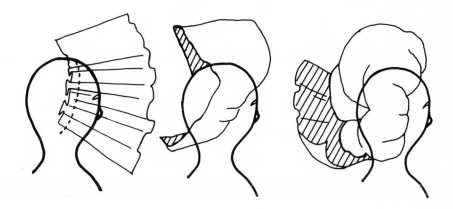

Figure 18. The hair for "Nurse" was made by sewing gathered cotton fabric to the head as shown here. The fabric was drawn to the back of the head, stuffed with Dacron batting, and then stitched down.

The nose of the "Egyptian Girl" (Plate 54) is also of interest. A piece of cardboard or other stiffener is used to form the basic nose shape. Fabric is then pulled over it and sewn. A chain stitch fills in the white of each eye and a button forms each iris.

The homey character of "Nurse" contrasts strongly with the rigid quality of "Egyptian Girl" and the delicate nature of the Renaissance Faire doll in Plate 55. Such contrasts will be apparent throughout the book; so will certain similarities.

The Renaissance Faire doll achieves subtlety not only by its finely embroidered face but by its magnificent hairdo. Though natural hair, which is used in this doll, is perhaps the material that first comes to mind, hair can be suggested with an amazing variety of materials. As you look through this book at various photographs, you will find ingenious ways of using different materials for hair.

Plate 54. "Egyptian Girl" from the collection of Helen Trimble. The nose is stiff paper covered with fabric. The hair is raffia-like material and chain-stitching suggests the white of the eyes.

Plate 55. Doll from the Los Angeles Renaissance Faire. Real hair streams down her back, and details of the face are embroidered. Clothing is partly sewn, partly tied in place.

Yarn is a common material that is handled in many ways to form hair. It may be used by the whole skein, as in "Maxine" (page 122), or as in the detailed coiffure of "Lady Astride a Ram" (Plate 56). Yarn loops may be sewn directly to the head (Figure 19, A), or they may be attached with a separate thread (Figure 19, B). Lengths of yarn may be sewn onto the head with a line of stitches down the back; the yarn is then drawn forward into the desired hairdo and tacked into place (Figure 20). The strands of yarn may be stitched to the top of the head or the sides (Figure 21) instead of to the back. There are many variations of this approach, and in working with yarns you will devise ways of producing whatever hairdo you desire. The homemade Raggedy Ann in Plate 57 also suggests a way of using yarn as hair.

Plate 56. Face of "Lady Astride a Ram" by Susan Morrison (full view in Color Plate 9). The hat, the hair style and the face all contribute to the doll's prim character.

Fabrics cut into different shapes can also be used to suggest hair. "Lazy Lily" (page 42) shows hair made from narrow strips of cloth. These strips are sewn and turned but are not stuffed (Figure 22). The open end of each form is then turned under and sewn to the head. Curls can be done in the same way by first sewing the desired curves and shapes. Care must be taken that these do not become so tiny that they cannot easily be turned inside out.

Figure 22. Strips of fabric may be sewn, then turned, and stitched into place as hair. A variation of this is to cut the fabric in a curved shape, adding a curl to the hair.

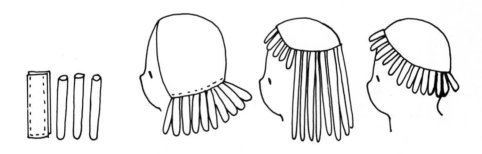

Figure 23. Tiny strips, when stuffed, make little round curls of hair. These can be sewn to a piece of cloth shaped to cover the head like a cap, which is then attached to the head as shown. Care must be taken not to make these strips too narrow to be turned right side out after they are sewn.

Stuffing the pieces of fabric provides another method for making hair. Kathy Glascock's "Brown-Faced Doll" (Plate 58) uses small tubes of stuffed fabric. These are sewn to a flat piece of fabric covering the head (Figure 23). The stuffed tubes stand out as round curls.

Plate 58. "Brown-Faced Doll" by Kathy Fukami Glascock. Of special interest in this doll is the hair, made from small, stuffed tubes of fabric. The detailed hands are also noteworthy.

Fur is a favorite hair material for Carol Ann Marsh's portrait dolls. (See "Grand-mother" and "Grandfather," page 14 and Color Plates 16 and 17.) Other materials used to imitate hair are raffia, unspun wool, strips of felt, paint, ball fringe, and common fringes. There are no limitations. Anything is acceptable if it suits your personal needs. Glee Masumoto made the hair for her "Mae West" doll (Plate 59) out of string. She dipped the string in a white glue, wrapped it around a plastic marking pen, and let it dry. These curls are combined with straight strands of yarn, and a feather tops off the "show girl" hairdo.

The face of the "Mae West" doll is shaped from a stuffed stocking. The soft structure allows the features to be formed by pinching various parts of the face together with stitches. This method has so many possibilities, it is described more fully in the next chapter.

9.

STOCKING-FACE DOLLS

Plate 60. "Woman" (detail) by the author. A stocking-face doll with pulled stitches to form nose and mouth. Gray yarn is used for eyebrows and hair, with large sequins for eyes.

Among the most expressive, most human, and funniest dolls are those with stocking faces. In these dolls the features are formed by stitching through the soft fabric and part of the stuffing inside. There are various approaches to creating this kind of face, and each craftsman or artist will discover what methods work best for him.

The head can be made from any soft fabric with some give to it—a jersey mesh, soft cotton, etc. Sew the material into a tubular form and gather it at the top (Figure 24). Turn the form and stuff it with cotton or Dacron batting or with kapok. The resulting head is then covered with a nylon stocking or similar fabric. Tie the stocking-covered head at the neck, letting some of the stuffing come below the line where you tie it off.

The stitching, which produces the features by pulling part of the face together, is now added so that it goes through both layers of material, catching part of the stuffing under the stitches. The face emerges as you sew, surprising you as it comes into focus through the fabric. It may seem to assert a presence and to indicate to you how the remaining features should be developed.

You need a good, strong thread for this, such as heavy-duty sewing thread, a waxed thread, or double strand of sewing thread. For working on a small head (about the size of a tennis ball), any standard needle will be adequate. If the doll's head is large, the needle will of course have to be longer. Use a darning needle.

The details of a stocking face show clearly in the close-up of "Woman" (Plate 60). Experimenting with these stitches is the best way to learn how to control them. You can always try a few stitches, pull them tight, and if the results are not satisfying, clip and pull the stitches out. It actually takes very few stitches to form or suggest the features. It is merely a matter of practice until you can form the face as you wish.

The body for the head can be an extension of the basic tube form, with arms and legs added, or it can be made separately and attached. Some doll makers use a "backbone" or armature, such as a piece of wire or a rod of wood, inserted into the head and neck to help hold the figure upright.

"Woman" (Plate 61) has a tin-can armature. The extra tubing below the doll's neck was inserted at the top of the can and pulled through to emerge from the bottom (Figure 25). The fabric was drawn up over the outside surface and taped in place. That held the head secure and upright. Then the can was padded and covered with fabric on the outside to form the body. Separate arms and additional fabric for clothing were attached to the shoulder and neck portion of the doll extending from the can.

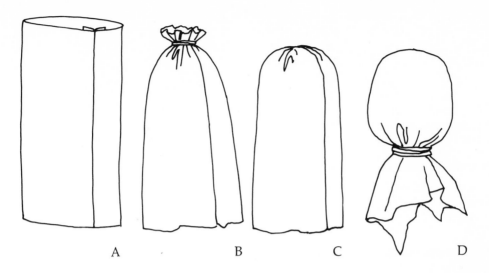

A   B   C   D

Figure 24. Tubular forms are made with one seam joining a rectangular piece of material (A). The tube is tied at the top (B). The gathered top can be used to suggest hair, or it can be hidden by turning the form as in C. In either case, the tube is stuffed with batting or kapok and the head shape is then tied, as in D.

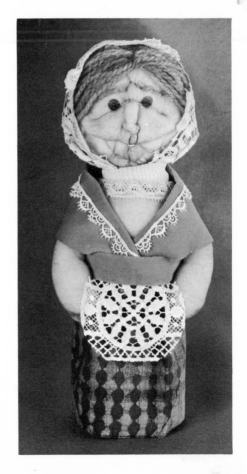

Plate 61. Full view of "Woman." Body has a tin-can armature. Arms are added but not legs. Height 11 inches.

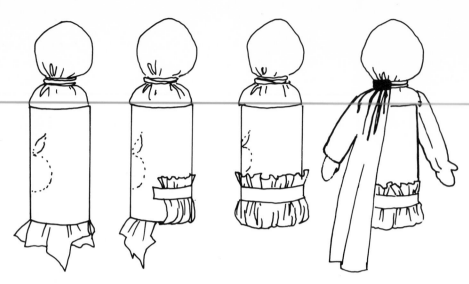

Figure 25. An orange juice can provides a framework for the doll's body. The basic tube-form of the stuffed head was extended and pulled through the can. The material was fastened around the lower edge of the can with masking tape. Arms and clothing were sewn to the neck and shoulder portions of the tube above the can. Padding between the can and the costume makes the body soft and doll-like.

Plate 62. "Debutante" by the author. Stuffed cotton stocking forms the face and the body, with no armature. Features are embroidered. Hair is stitched yarn. Height 9 inches.

However, I find that just firm stuffing is usually adequate. No armature was used for "Debutante" (Plate 62). Embroidery was added to the face to define the eyes, brows, and mouth.

The stocking face can be made by stuffing Dacron batting directly inside a section of nylon hose, with no other fabric base used for the head. (See the "Chaperone" doll in Color Plate 14.) In cutting the nylon, be sure to allow enough extra to avoid "runs." Leave it tubular, and it can be gathered at the top and bottom, as in Figure 24. The more heavily woven section at the top of a stocking was used to suggest the "Chaperone" doll's hair.

A collection of dolls by the late Emelia Casada shows a dramatic and powerful use of this stitched-stocking method. "The Old Woman" (Plate 63a) combines several stitching methods. The material of the face is tucked or folded to form the mouth, and nylon is pulled over it. The nose was also formed in the basic fabric before being covered by nylon, and sequins were added for the eyes.

Plate 63a. "Old Woman" by Emelia Casada. Stocking-face doll with black sequin eyes and velvet hat. The brown paper shopping bag is in keeping with her gloomy appearance. Height 13 inches.

Pencil lines further emphasize the features. The somber and somewhat menacing nature of the old woman is heightened by her heavy black clothes and the bullet used as a button. A similar facial construction was used on her work "Matador" (Plate 63b and Color Plate 15). The matador's mouth is a fold sewn into the cloth of the basic head; the nylon is pulled over and left smooth. The stitching of the nose, however, catches both layers of fabric to create the form. The ears are smaller, nylon-covered, stuffed shapes. Buttons form the eyes, and the full figure is shown in its elaborate costume on page 56.

From what I could learn of Emelia Casada's work, her dolls were all portraits of friends or people she knew. They are vivid and strong. "Lady" (Plate 64) shows details of stitching over the stocking. Lead pencil has again been used to add depth and lines. All of these dolls are meticulously dressed and they vary in size from 13 inches to 32 inches tall.

Plate 63b. "Matador" (detail) by Emelia Casada, from the author's collection. The mouth is a fold sewn into the material of the doll's face. These stitches do not go through the nylon stocking that covers the face, though the stitches that form the nose do. Staring button eyes and eyeglasses seem marvelously incongruous with the activities of the matador.

Plate 64. "Lady" by Emelia Casada. This portrait doll uses a stocking face with stitched features, emphasized by embroidery and pencil lines. The hair is suggested with netting. Doll is 21 inches high.

Plate 65. Doll from Martinique (detail). The head is very tightly stuffed; material is stiffened. Nose is sculptured by stitching, ears are added, and other features are embroidered.

Plate 66. Doll from Martinique, from the author's collection. Textured fabric of the face is used for the body as well. Hands are constructed with individually made fingers. Height 23 inches.

The stitching technique of the stocking face can be used without the nylon covering and combined with other methods of forming features. A doll from Martinique (Plates 65 and 66) has a magnificently shaped head of textured fabric. The full, rounded jaw is very firm, and the material was probably starched or stiffened in some way. Perhaps a sizing was applied to the head after it was shaped and stuffed. The nose and mouth are formed with pulled stitches, but the ears are added separately. The doll is very well constructed, sturdy and packed tight with stuffing. Incredible detail is achieved in the hands (Plate 66). Each finger is made separately, and the stuffed forms are sewn into the stuffed fabric that forms the palm and the back of the hand.

Other examples of the potential for dramatic portrayal with the stocking-face technique are provided by Carol Ann Marsh, whose dolls are among the best sewn anywhere. She arrived at the use of this process by herself, as did Emelia

Casada and others. Each was making the best use of the materials available. Carol Ann Marsh writes about her own work, "Making the dolls is a great joy to me, but the finished work is the real satisfaction. No amount of money replaces the chuckles one feels the many times one looks at the 'silly' things."

Her "Lady of Easy Virtue" (Plate 67) is a masterful characterization. The coarse face, the stocky figure, and the coat—with membership pin and the unlikely combination of fur and tweed—all result from keen observation and an ability to combine all these elements forcefully. The artist makes you laugh out loud and yet feel compassion at the same time.

Among the most human and lovable dolls are Carol Ann's portraits of her grandparents. (Color Plates 16 and 17, and page 14). The postures, details of clothing, prints and patterns selected all complement the candid expressions on the faces.

The pulled-stitch technique, applied to stocking-covered or other fabric faces, offers a great range of creative possibilities for the doll maker, especially in the realm of personal comments in sculptural form. Because this approach allows such complexities of expression, anyone seriously pursuing doll making will eventually want to work with it.

Plate 67. "Lady of Easy Virtue" by Carol Ann Marsh. This marvelous stocking-face figure reveals the artist's ability to observe, select, and depict those details essential to such a powerful characterization. No armature is used, just kapok stuffing. Height 21 inches.

10.

KNITTED & WOVEN DOLLS

Plate 68. *"Stocking Doll" by the author. A ready-made cotton sock is stuffed to form this doll. The bunting is lined fabric. Height 14 inches.*

Knitted and Woven Dolls

Just as stockings of knitted nylon or cotton served to make facial forms, similar materials—preformed or hand-knitted—can be readily and easily utilized for the entire doll. For simple dolls, socks are the most available source, and these make especially good, soft dolls for children. Cotton, wool or synthetics work equally well, and all come in a wide range of colors.

"Stocking Doll" (Plate 68) uses the foot of a sock for the head and body of the doll. The body is stuffed, then tied at the neck (Figure 26). No arms and legs are added; there is just a soft "wad" of body. The doll is tied at the bottom, and yarn hair is sewn in place on the head portion. Button eyes and embroidered details are added to the face. The bunting, made from an arch-shaped piece of cloth, is tied around the doll with yarn. This doll is cuddly and soft and suggests the form of a baby.

Plate 69. "Baby," a stocking doll by the author. Simply and easily made from one sock. It is stuffed with Dacron batting. Seated, 5 inches.

A more detailed version of this construction is seen in "Baby" (Plate 69), made from a child's sock. This doll is so simple that one can be completed in half an hour. Figure 27 shows how to proceed. Cut the ribbed portion of the sock off to be used for a cap and as arms. Use the toe as the head, letting the heel of the sock provide a "seat" so that the doll will sit upright. To form the head, stuff the toe of the sock and then tie it where the doll's neck will be.

Figure 26. The cotton sock or anklet in an adult's size can be stuffed and tied to suggest a doll-form, as shown. Almost any fiber will do.

Figure 27. A child's sock (size 2 to 4) can be made into a doll by first cutting the ribbed end off, as shown. Then the head is stuffed and tied, and a slit is made to form the legs. Body and legs are stuffed, then sewn shut. The ribbed portion of the sock is then cut in half horizontally. The top half with the decorative or finished edge is kept for a cap. The remainder is halved vertically to make two arms (a and b). Sew the arms as shown by dotted lines and attach them to the body. Add the cap and features.

Plate 70. "Snake Lady" by the author. Tubular knit forms the basic body structure. Features are felt appliqué and embroidery, and a stocking top forms the hair. Total length 28 inches.

When the head is tied, stuff the body and make a short slit to separate the legs. Then slip-stitch the legs shut, adding a final bit of stuffing to them as you sew. Dacron batting will make the doll soft and washable. The sock's ribbed portion, which was cut away, is now cut horizontally in half. The uppermost half of the ribbed portion, with its finished or decorative edge, is used for a cap. It sits like a crown over the head. The other half of the ribbed portion is cut into two lengths and sewn to make arms. Sew the two lengths, turn and stuff them, then slip-stitch them to the body. A belt, in this case yarn, was tied on.

Clothing can be suggested with buttons and tied yarn, or separate clothes can be made. Facial details are embroidered. The idea for this doll can be adapted to making a doll from a larger sock as well. This would probably require two socks in order to have enough ribbing for both the arms and legs. As the body gets longer, the arms and legs also get proportionately longer. The legs would be sewn like the arms and inserted at the open end of the stuffed body, which would then be sewn shut.

Using the sock form is an excellent way to begin a doll, since the body is so easily fashioned from it. The basic structure is often the most cumbersome aspect for a beginning doll maker. Once that is solved, adding the details of features and clothes is easily accomplished. These stocking dolls are all great favorites of children. Use them as a starting point, adding your own variations.

"Snake Lady," (Plate 70) is made from a hand-knitted, stocking-like tubular shape. The doll, partially stuffed, suggests possibilities for forms other than the human figure. Felt and embroidery are used for the features, and the head is stuffed and tied.

Hand-knitting the basic doll-form allows a high degree of creativity. Sonja Pimentel uses her knitting needles like drawing pens to produce her dolls. The figures are knitted, then stuffed. In "Shakespeare" (Plate 71), a variety of common knitting stitches was used. The yarn hair was added afterwards and the details of the face are yarn embroidery.

Plate 71. "Shakespeare" by Sonja Pimentel of Sausalito, Calif. The detailed figure is hand-knitted with a variety of common stitches. About 28 inches.

Plate 72. "Three Kings" by Sonja Pimentel. Simple shapes are given complexity through the knitted patterns. The faces are embroidered over the knitting. Height 8 inches.

"Three Kings" (Plate 72) are other examples of her delightful use of the knitted form. They are simpler in shaping than the "Shakespeare," but the patterns woven into the clothing give them a feeling of detail and complexity. Faces are again wool embroidery, hair is added, and the crowns are separate, knitted forms.

"Homage to Crow Agency" (Plate 73) by Bucky King is hand-woven of wool and white deer-hide strips. The materials, techniques, and stylized human form are reminiscent of the Indian culture without being imitative. The figure is symbolic rather than individualized.

Any ready-made woven or knitted form, such as a stocking, has certain limitations already in its structure, whereas knitting or weaving your own forms by hand gives you greater control over them. In making dolls, you must decide if the advantages of ready-made shapes offset the limitations imposed by them. This is governed in part by the purpose of the doll. It is hard to imagine, for example, that the concept in Bucky King's doll, where the reference is so specific, could have been carried out with preformed materials. However, in a little doll for a child, where expediency, ease of structure, and washability may be essential, perhaps it would be silly to use anything other than the stocking. So it becomes essentially a matter of choosing the approach and the material which is best or most appropriate for the specific needs of the artist or of the recipient.

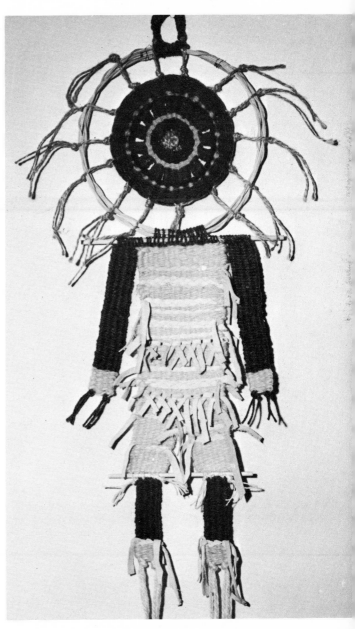

Plate 73. "Homage to Crow Agency" by Bucky King. The construction of hand-woven wool with deer-hide strips is in keeping with the Indian culture to which it pays tribute. (Photo by W. S. King.)

11.

OTHER MATERIALS FOR DOLLS

Plate 74. "Leather Dolls" by Ron Coviello of San Francisco, Calif. A combination of leather and felt is used. The felt of the faces is covered with several coats of gesso, then pencil and paint are applied. Height is 8 inches.

Other Materials for Dolls

Leather, nuts, shells, iron-on tape, batiked or silk-screened fabrics, apples, dough, and papier-mâché are all appropriate materials for doll making. If any particular one serves your purpose and meets your needs, then use it. Everything from corn husks to bread crumbs has been used and is acceptable. Included in this chapter are some of these approaches which are not easily categorized but which further expand the field of doll making.

Leather, which is a flexible and durable material, comes in a great variety of natural and dyed colors. Scraps, which are inexpensive, are often available at hobby shops, sandal shops, upholsterers, decorators and thrift shops. The best source is a tannery, if you have one located near you. The dolls in Plate 74 are a combination of leather and felt, stitched and stuffed. The hair is made up of strips of felt. The felt faces are drawn and painted.

Each facial area was first given several coats of gesso (glue with whiting). Gesso remains somewhat flexible and tends not to crack when bent or moved. When several layers of gesso are applied, the white coating becomes opaque, and the texture of the felt is covered with a smooth surface, especially if the gesso is sanded lightly between coats. Then pencil, watercolor or marking pen can be used to delineate the features. The painted felt surface is one option. However, the felt itself can, to some extent, be formed.

By placing felt over a projection, such as over a bowl turned upside down, and then applying steam, the felt can be shaped. It is like blocking an old felt hat. Further moistening and stretching or forcing makes it possible to press the felt into various shapes. Some commercially manufactured doll faces are made by placing felt over a modeled form, then shrinking the felt over the model.

Another means of making the face is to shape papier-mâché over a clay model. First the face is sculptured in soft clay. Then this clay form is coated with liquid green soap or with a lotion or cream to prevent the mâché from sticking. Strips of paper, torn rather than cut, are then dipped into a wheat paste, about the consistency of cream. The strips are laid over the clay face until enough thickness is built up for the paper to hold its shape. When the mâché is dry, the resulting face shell is lifted from the clay form.

You can also build up an entire papier-mâché head by using a ball-shaped armature to begin with. An orange will do, or a Styrofoam ball. It depends upon the desired size of the finished head. Or you can wad up paper, fastening it with masking tape to form a ball. Once this ball is covered with strips of the papier-mâché, features can be added by pinching the paper together or by adding extra paper in some areas. (See Figure 28.)

When the papier-mâché is hard and dry it is ready to finish, unless the armature is an orange or other perishable goods. If you have used an orange, cut the head in half with a utility knife and remove the orange. When the orange is out, place the two shells of mâché back together and overlap additional pieces of papier-mâché to cover the joint. A neck can be added by placing a section of cardboard tubing beneath the spherical head. Fresh strips of mâché are then used to connect the head and neck.

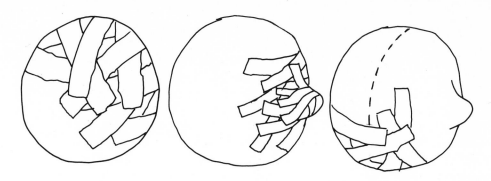

Figure 28. Papier-mâché strips can be applied to the surface of a Styrofoam ball to build up a head. An extra wad of mâché can be added for the nose; the damp paper can be pinched to produce features. If the core is of perishable material, as an orange, cut mâché form in half, remove core, and glue shells back together with strips of papier-mâché.

When thoroughly dry, the head can be coated with layers of gesso until it is smooth. Sanding between coats will make it smoother. The gesso can then be painted in detail. Hands and feet can also be made of papier-mâché. The mâché can be coated with a latex paint, though this will not smooth the surface as the gesso does. If poster paints are used over the base coating, a finishing protective film of spray should be used.

The poetic and charming dolls made by Kathy Fukami Glascock and shown in Plates 75 and 76 have papier-mâché heads. Though she also works with all-fabric dolls (as seen in Plates 22 and 58), she makes beautiful use of the papier-mâché. The dolls' faces have reserve and dignity, further emphasized by their tranquil poses and simple clothing. Kathy Glascock handles the painted details of the face with a sure and delightful touch.

Papier-mâché is the primary material used by Carol Anthony to create her extraordinary gallery of characters, such as "Russell," the All-American Anti-Hero (Plate 77). Carol describes him as "the neighbor down the street who took off to the corner Deli-Bar to watch the Red Sox on the tube for a while." Full of gross exaggerations, he is a marvelous embodiment of both the familiar and the absurd.

Papier-mâché as a medium can remain very simple, as it has in Kathy Fukami Glascock's dolls, or it can be carried to the complexity of detail and structure shown in Carol Anthony's incredible creatures. Anyone interested in working with this material should seek more specific information, and there are many good books available on papier-mâché.

Though seldom used, another available material which has many possibilities is iron-on tape. It comes in a good variety of colors and it is fast and easy to apply. Its use has already been seen in Plates 33 and 34. "Maxine" (Plate 78) is another example of its application for facial detail. The features were cut from different colored tapes, and the cutouts were ironed onto the fabric before the head-form was sewn together, turned and stuffed. A full skein of yarn was pulled over the head to make the hair, and the yarns were then tacked into place with thread.

Plate 75. Lady in a Blue Dress" by Kathy Fukami Glascock. A stuffed fabric body is attached to the papier-mâché head. The features are painted onto the gesso-coated face. About 9 inches. (Photo by Baylis Glascock.)

Plate 76. "Girl with Bow in Hair" by Kathy Fukami Glascock. Face of painted papier-mâché is poetic and serene. Doll has a stuffed-fabric body. (Photo by Baylis Glascock.)

Plate 78. "Maxine" by the author. Iron-on tape is used to show features on this fabric face. A full skein of yarn is attached to the head and arranged as hair. Head is 7 inches.

"Tarzan" (Plate 79) has iron-on tape to show the hair on his chest as well as to define his features. Remember that the tape must be ironed on while the fabric is still flat. The hair on Tarzan's head is sewn from brown velvet, stuffed as it is stitched.

Elizabeth Fuller's dolls, shown in Plates 80 and 81, use the batik process. Batik is a wax-resist method, and any of several basic approaches will work. There are several excellent books available on batik, and you should consult one if you've never handled this process before. Basically, wax (paraffin and beeswax) is painted onto parts of a fabric to make it waterproof in the areas that are not to be dyed. When the fabric is dyed with cold-water or room-temperature dyes, these painted areas resist the dye. The process can continue through many dye baths, depending upon the desired result in pattern and color. A simplified way of using the batik process is described in the chapter Transferring Children's Ideas into Dolls. The process used by Mrs. Fuller is more complex and more permanent, and allows for greater detail and variation.

Silk-screening is also useful in doll making, especially where a number of dolls are to be reproduced. Plate 82 shows some very simple dolls which are screened on felt. Body colors vary, as do the paints, suggesting an overall array of color greater than just the one color on another (Color Plate 4). Silk-screening is simply another means of stencil printing. Again, the process is one which must be pursued in other references if you have not screened before. For readers who are already familiar with the process, doll making offers a new use.

Plate 79. *"Tarzan," a fabric doll with iron-on tape, by the author. Hair is brown velvet. 13 inches high.*

Plate 80. *"Byzantine Dolls" by Elizabeth Fuller of Claremont, Calif. Faces and costumes are created by the batik process. Feet and arms are sewn and stuffed separately and inserted in the seam of the combined body-form. Height about 9 inches.*

Plate 81. *"Mermaid" by Elizabeth Fuller. The rich textural variation is the result of the wax-resist process used in batik.*

Plate 82. "Flat Pat," silk-screened dolls on felt, designed by the author. Height 11 inches.

Dolls made from edible materials give unusual results. One example by Mrs. Dorothy Pollock utilizes crumbs (Plate 83). The almost translucent look of the face is achieved with the unlikely combination of dry bread crumbs and glue (a wheat paste). Mrs. Pollock has no set recipe; the two ingredients are merely mixed to a consistency that can be handled and molded. A wire or dowel can be inserted before the head dries in order to have some means of later connecting the body to the head.

Another of Mrs. Pollock's works, "Annie's Apple Grannie" (Plate 84), uses an apple for the head. This is a traditional doll-form. To do this, you must have a good, firm apple. (A Delicious will do nicely, or use any fairly hard, eating apple.) Part of the peeling must be cut away for the face. All of the peeling can be removed, if you like, or some can be left on to suggest hair. The features are carved into the face, with slits for the eyes and the mouth. As the apple dries, it assumes new shapes. There is no way to know just how the face is going to turn out. Features may be added with bits of peeling set into the raw apple before it dries. Rice may also be inserted into the mouth to suggest teeth.

The apple must dry *slowly*, and dry weather is best for this. An oven heated with a pilot light provides good drying. But do not place the apple in a "low" oven. If the apple bakes, or even partially cooks, it is more likely to make a rotten mess than an apple-head doll.

Plate 83. "Crumb Doll" by Dorothy Pollock of Concord, Calif. A mixture of dried bread crumbs and glue forms the head of this doll. Tiny white beads were inserted for teeth. Height 8 inches.

Plate 84. "Annie's Apple Grannie" by Dorothy Pollock. This is a traditional doll made by carving and drying an apple for the head. Height 11 inches.

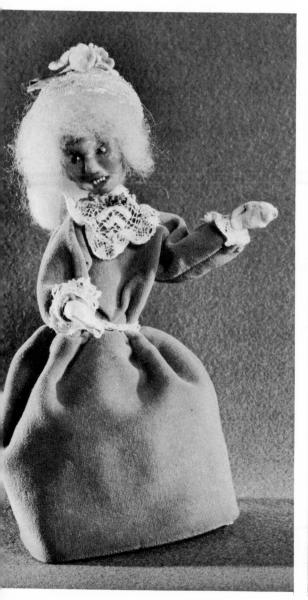

Plate 85. "Hammerhead Doll" by Helen Trimble. Head and body are stuffed fabric, but arms and legs are made of twine. About 9 inches.

Helen Trimble's little "Hammerhead Doll" (Plate 85) uses twine for arms and legs. A similar treatment is used by Nancy Greaver for her "Sling Doll" (Plate 86). The arms and legs are one long cord, tied to suggest feet and hands. There is no body to the doll other than the cord covered by a dress. It is, as the name suggests, a perfect doll for a child to "sling." Figure 29 shows how the "Sling Doll" is assembled.

Nuts and shells and the dried cores of fruits and vegetables provide further variations for dolls. Included here are just two of the many examples available. One is an Ozark doll (Plate 87) whose face is a piece of corncob. The other, a little Danish doll (Plate 88), has a filbert for the head and a pine cone as shawl. Walnuts, acorns, hickory nuts, corn husks, and pebbles are among the materials which can be used.

Plate 86. "Sling Doll" by Nancy Greaver. Arms and legs are made from one long tube of fabric filled with cording. The head is pieced and stuffed. Both appliqué and embroidery are used in defining features. Length about 14 inches.

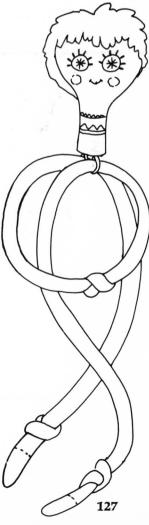

Figure 29. The sling doll has no body at all. The arms and legs are one long cord, knotted to indicate hands and attached to the base of the head. Clothing is then attached to the neck.

Plate 87. "Corncob Doll," a traditional doll from the Ozarks, has a section of corncob for the face, with a kernel of corn inserted for the nose. Seated, 7 inches high.

Plate 88. "Nut and Pine Cone Doll." A filbert is used as the head in this little Danish doll. A pine cone forms the shawl, and stiffened burlap is used for the skirt. Height 4 inches.

Plate 89. "Methuselah," a finger puppet of felt by the author. Hollow-bodied doll is animated by index finger. Embroidery floss forms the hair, and the eyes and nose are stitched on. Height 5 inches.

Figure 30. Hand puppets are larger than finger puppets, and the thumb and middle finger may be used to manipulate the arms. Finger puppets are made to just fit over the ends of the fingers, and several may be used on one hand at a time.

Finger puppets are hollow-bodied dolls that are completed by the fingers inserted to animate them. "Methuselah" (Plate 89) is one such puppet. Others are "Nickolos and Nastasha" (Color Plate 10) and "Rapunzel" (Color Plate 13). These are used on the index finger, or the middle finger. On larger finger puppets (or hand puppets) the middle finger and the thumb may provide movement for the arms. This is illustrated in Figure 30.

The simplest way to begin the puppet is to cut a combined head-and-neck shape from a double layer of felt. These two shapes are sewn together and stuffed; the body and details are added to that form. Figure 31 shows the steps in putting the finger puppet together. Finger puppets are especially adaptable for storytelling, and children of all ages are delighted by them.

Figure 31. Finger puppets may be started by cutting head and neck from felt. Cut two identical pieces and sew. Stuff lightly. The body should be large enough to slip over a finger. Measure by rolling a piece of felt around one finger to assure proper fit. Features and hair can then be added, along with details of the clothing.

12.

OTHER DIRECTIONS

Plate 90. "Portrait of Dr. Sims" by Michael Learned of Santa Rosa, Calif. Silk-screened print on fabric, stuffed to produce a bust. Height about 13 inches.

Other Directions

Working with human figures in three-dimensional stuffed fabric or other common materials has tremendous potential for artists and craftsmen. It is sometimes difficult to set a dividing line between doll making and sculpture. Purposeful communication has been one criterion for sculpture, but as some of the examples in this book indicate dolls can also fulfill this function. One distinction that can be made, however, is that objects made of fabric or papier-mâché have less intrinsic value than those made of bronze or marble and so are less apt to be thought of in terms of permanent works of art seeking profundity. Some doll makers refer to their work as "soft sculpture," some as "people figures" and some simply as "dolls." Fortunately, most doll makers care little about how they are labeled. They are too engrossed in creative production to spend much time and concern over categorizing their work.

Though doll makers do not take their creations over-seriously, this is not to say that doll makers are not serious about their work. They do not engage in discussions of aesthetic attributes but instead let their creations speak for themselves. It is the human quality of the dolls, with which we identify, that makes us laugh at their pompousness or smile at their being so full of our own conceits and inadequacies. We see ourselves and *must* laugh. They put us in perspective.

There is a vital interest in doll making today. It is an area still being explored, but the possibilities already discovered prove its worth as an artistic medium. Dolls seem to be particularly suited as deflators of human self-assurance. Perhaps their greatest value is in their ability to make us laugh and enjoy our own faults and foibles.

Plate 91. "Four at the Table" by Lenore Davis. The busts are of velveteen with painted faces. All are stitched and stuffed. Brown chair lines are painted directly onto the figures. Heads, 7 inches high. (Photo by Lenore Davis.)

Plate 92. "Chair Lady" by Lenore Davis. Chair and figure merge in the black-and-white checkered cotton form. The felt face is machine-embroidered. Height 10 inches. (Photo by Lenore Davis.)

The "Portrait of Dr. Sims" (Plate 90) by Michael Learned is similar in concept to the work of many Pop artists. This portrait is silk-screened on fabric and the stuffed form is almost life sized. It has a flat, solid base so that it sits upright and it is elevated by a column to the lofty position of a marble bust. This marvelous soft-form bust pokes wonderful fun at pomposity and pretense. Our response to its absurdity is similar to that evoked by Claes Oldenburg's giant soft-form Pop sculptures of hamburgers and other glorified trivia of American life.

The various doll-forms used by Lenore Davis are pointing toward other new directions. The human form does not limit her manipulation of spatial elements. In her composite-body dolls, such as "Four at the Table" (Plate 91), she collects anywhere from two to a dozen or more figures and treats them as a unit. The chairs, painted on the back of each stuffed form, are also treated as part of the entire form.

In "Chair Lady" (Plate 92), the human form and furniture merge into one three-dimensional form, expressing an interplay between the figure and its surroundings that is reminiscent of a Steinberg drawing. The doll-form is freed of restrictions and anything becomes possible. "Moth Woman" (Plate 93) combines the human form with delicate, machine-embroidered wings.

Plate 93. "Moth Woman" by Lenore Davis. Orange velveteen body, white organdy wings with machine embroidery, stuffed. Antique crochet is used on the body. Height 13 inches. (Photo by Lenore Davis.)

Plate 94. "My Marlboro Man" by Carol Anthony. A deliciously wry comment on advertising. Constructed of papier-mâché and fabric. Height 4 feet. (Photo by Becky Young.)

The figures created by Carol Anthony illustrate the difficulty of distinguishing between doll-forms and sculpture. Whichever category they may fall into, the fact that they are devastatingly humorous comments on human existence is unquestionable.

"My Marlboro Man" (Plate 94) is constructed of papier-mâché, fabric, fur, hair, and some ready-made articles. Subtitled "Walter and His Chocolate Horse," the figure stands about 4 feet high. Here Carol Anthony has taken the stereotyped Western Heroic He-Man, astride his horse and with all the proper trappings, and brought him down to human size.

About "The Madame" in Plate 95, Carol Anthony says, "She is the 50-year-old proprietor and keeper of the girls at the Orleans House of Sin. Still going strong for her years and build." About her work in general, she adds, "I do caricatures of the Middle-American Anti-Hero in 3-D from papier-mâché and assorted Salvation Army and Morgan Memorial remnants." Another of her dolls, "Beach Honey," is shown in Color Plate 1.

"Helen Resurrected" (Plate 96), by M. Nelson Hooton, also contrasts the heroic and the comically human. The doll is 4 feet long. With her serious expression and austere profile, "Helen" assumes some of the dignity of Helen of Troy, for whom she was named. Some of that queenly trait disappears, however, in the appearance of the chubby legs. The elaborate hairdo and the gracefully long neck cannot overcome the beautiful incongruity of those legs. She is at once a vision of royal elegance and of the woman-next-door.

Many doll figures present a most unglamorized aspect of portraiture. Carol Ann Marsh's "Woman of Easy Virtue" (page 107) and "Portrait of a Woman" (Plate 97) are examples. Each doll is a concentrated collection of human characteristics found in other people familiar to us. We have all seen someone with similar traits somewhere. The doll rings an insistent bell of recognition for some detail of her stance or build, or for her appearance or expression. Certainly Carol Ann's work is a departure from the ordinary concept of dolls.

Susan Morrison, whose jointed dolls appear throughout this book, must also be recognized for her departure from any stereotyped notion of doll making. Her combinations of animal forms with human ones are unique in concept and exquisite in execution.

Doll making is as expressive a medium as any other in the arts. The materials are so common and the methods so customary that it is easy to overlook the extremely perceptive and provocative comments made by doll makers. They produce intuitively, and are totally absorbed in their work. There is often an intense personal involvement without concern for public acceptance or popular opinion. Therefore, in contrast to much contemporary painting or sculpture, few dolls are made for public galleries or exhibitions, but doll making does provide one more means through which we can offer an individual viewpoint on the world about us.

Plate 95. "The Madame" by Carol An-thony. *Papier-mâché, fabric and ready-made articles are ingeniously arranged into a real "presence." (Photo by Becky Young.)*

Plate 96. "Helen Resurrected" by M. Nelson Hooton. *An elaborate hairdo, long neck and embroidered features give regal stature which is deliberately di-minished by the chubby legs of this kapok-stuffed fabric doll. Height 4 feet.*

Plate 97. "Portrait of a Woman" by Carol Ann Marsh. *The contrast between the somber expression and the gay bril-liance of the blouse gives the doll a pathetic quality. The figure is stuffed with kapok and has a stitched stocking face. Height 9 inches.*

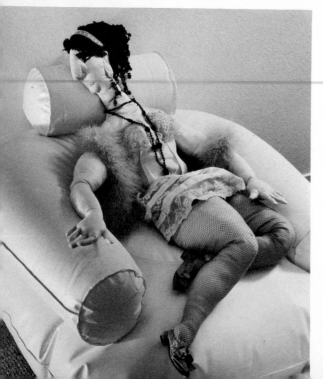